D0506056

STORIES FROM THE ILIAD
AND THE ODYSSEY

TITLES IN THIS SERIES:

MYTHS AND LEGENDS

STORIES FROM THE ILIAD AND ODYSSEY

G. CHANDON

Edited and translated from the French
by Barbara Whelpton

Illustrated by René Péron

BURKE LONDON

© BURKE PUBLISHING COMPANY LTD. 1964

First published in the English language September 1964
Reprinted February 1968

Translated and adapted from *Contes et récits tirés de l'Iliade et de l'Odyssée*
© Fernard Nathan 1962

222   69218   9   Library Ed.
222   69377   0   Schools Ed.

BURKE PUBLISHING COMPANY LIMITED
14 JOHN STREET   *   LONDON, W.C.1

SET IN MONOPHOTO BASKERVILLE
MADE AND PRINTED IN GREAT BRITAIN BY
WILLIAM CLOWES AND SONS, LIMITED, LONDON AND BECCLES

Contents

PART ONE
The Iliad

PART TWO
The Odyssey

List of Colour Plates

PART ONE

THE ILIAD

Introduction

We know little about Homer, who was the greatest of Greek poets and one of the greatest poets the world has ever known, though it seems probable that he lived about nine centuries before the birth of Christ.

So great was his fame that when Athens was the centre of the world's civilisation, a law was passed ordering that his poems should be recited in public from beginning to end on certain feast days.

The *Iliad* tells only half of the story of the great siege of Troy, which lasted, according to legend, for ten long years.

We do not even know if Troy really existed—though it is believed to have been near the mouth of the Dardanelles in a region which is now part of Turkey.

The war between the Greeks and the Trojans broke out because Paris, second son of Priam, King of Troy, eloped with Helen, wife of Menelaus, the King of Sparta, with whom he had been staying.

You must realise that the Greece of ancient days consisted of many little kingdoms, each of them centring round a city, such as Sparta, Mycenae and Thebes.

Most of the countless Greek islands were also ruled by kings, and there were settlements of Greeks on the shores of Asia Minor, of which Troy was probably one.

Now, Paris came from Asia Minor and was considered by the Greeks in Europe to be a barbarian, and so the fact that he ran away with the wife of the King of Sparta was considered to be doubly insulting.

Thus it was that the kings of Greece collected together under the leadership of King Agamemnon of Mycenae to force the Trojans to return Helen to her husband, and also the treasure that Paris had taken when he eloped.

The *Iliad* describes only some of the events of the siege of Troy, and in particular the rivalries between the champions of each nation. It is, in fact, called by some Greeks the story of the wrath of Achilles.

Other poets have described how Troy was finally captured by a cunning trick, by leaving outside the walls the great wooden horse in which the Greek chieftain, Ulysses, and some of his men were concealed.

When, at last, this horse was taken into the city, the warriors came out of their hiding-place and opened the gates to let in the remainder of the army, which had returned under the cover of darkness.

I

The Anger of Kings

USE, *sing to me of the wrath of Achilles, the fatal wrath which plunged the Greeks into the profoundest sorrow and caused the death of hundreds of heroes, leaving their bodies as carrion for dogs and vultures. Muse, sing to me of the great quarrel which set Agamemnon and Achilles against each other. . . .*

Homer's Introduction to the
Iliad

For nearly ten years the Greeks had been besieging Troy, the ancient and mighty city of Priam, descendant of Dardanus and ancestor of the Trojans Situated in the north-west of Asia Minor, it was so strongly fortified that the old King who had inherited this realm could walk upon his ramparts without fear for the future.

Now, on the far side of the sandy plain which separated the town from the sea, the army of the Greeks had encamped. They had come in their hundreds and thousands; their tents of saffron and gold rose up like another city and the masts of the twelve hundred vessels which had brought them to the Asian shore were outlined against the deep blue of the sea like the trees of a dark forest.

Ten years! Indeed, nearly ten years had passed since the Greeks had come to beleaguer the immense city of Priam. They had no catapults with which to shatter its walls; they could only hope to take it by starvation. But the besieged had filled their storehouses with grain, and had sturdily resolved to stand firm and defeat the Greeks by their doughty resistance. Willingly they accepted the sacrifices and privations demanded by their King and by the gods.

For the gods, the majestic gods of Olympus, lived among men, often sharing their joys and sorrows as well as their toil. From the crest of their lofty dwelling-place, hidden by the clouds, they watched unceasingly the corner of earth where the heroes of Greece and those of Troy were engaged in mortal combat, but the gods could not look on unmoved at the dramatic events unfolding before their eyes. Some were on the side of the Greeks and others favoured the Trojans, so, in the midst of Olympus itself, there were differences which aroused the greatest anger in the hearts of the deities.

Juno, bride of Jupiter the all-powerful, had become the ardent ally of the Greeks. She shared their hatred of the Trojans, against whom she also felt a personal animosity. The handsome Paris, one of the fifty sons of Priam, King of Troy, having been appointed to judge the contest of beauty between Juno, Minerva and Venus, had given the prize to Venus and had proclaimed her the most beautiful of all the goddesses. From that time on, Juno and Minerva had scorned the descendants of Dardanus, and, filled with wounded pride, they had done everything to help the Greeks.

As for Venus, she had wished to show her gratitude to Paris and had induced Mars, the god of war, to give his support to the Trojans, and Apollo, god of the sun, had joined them. The other inhabitants of Olympus watched this grievous quarrel between the gods, and they were filled with anxiety and perplexity. High above these warring gods and men, Jupiter, sovereign lord of life and death and master of the Universe, granted defeat or victory to either side according to his whim, for the fate and destiny of mankind were in his hands.

It is Jupiter, King of the gods, to whom men raised their prayers; Trojans and Greeks besought him with equal fervour by making sacrifices and burnt offerings. Thus for the past ten years clouds of incense had been rising up to Olympus from the altars of Troy and from the Greek altars built among the rocks on the shore.

It may well be that this Troy, known by Jupiter to be condemned to destruction by the relentless law of Fate, moved him by her heroic resistance. But, in spite of the pity which he felt for the subjects of the city of Priam, he would not save them from the tragic disaster which awaited them, from the punishment which the crime of Paris had deserved.

Paris, who had kindled the flame of discord between the gods, was also the cause of the mortal quarrel between men. Whilst staying in Greece at the Court of Menelaus, king of Sparta, he had abused the generous hospitality which he had received there. Taking advantage of the King's absence, he had carried away his host's bride, Helen, and plundered the treasure-house. Then, proud of this theft, he had returned to Troy with his captive and his booty. As soon as this vile deed came to be known, the whole of Greece rose up in anger.

Now the conquest of land and of its bounty had been the cause of many acts of violence in the past; indeed, the first conquerors of this land had been brigands, yet little by little they had ceased to plunder and kill. So it was that Paris, who had carried away a married woman and had stolen her husband's treasures, aroused the anger not only of the King whom he had wronged, but of the whole of Greece.

It was to avenge this insult that the Greeks had sent chosen warriors to the Trojan shore, determined to punish the culprit and his countrymen.

Just was the cause of Greece and just was her desire to make the guilty man expiate his crime. Therefore great Jupiter remained unshaken in his resolve, although he was filled with pity at the ultimate fate of the Trojans. Seated on his throne, resting his chin upon his hand, he watched, listened and pondered.

Great was the commotion in the Greek camp. Ten days previously, a priest of Apollo named Chryses had landed on the Trojan coast moaning and begging for mercy, for in one of their raids on the islands of the Ionian Sea whose peoples were allied to Priam, the Greeks had carried off many captives, among them Chryseis, daughter of Chryses, whom they had given to Agamemnon as his share of the booty.

Now, Agamemnon was supreme Commander of the Greek Army, and he was the brother of Menelaus. It was he who had scoured Greece, summoning the different kings to arms, after hearing of the fate of Helen, and these kings had chosen him as their leader. Belonging as he did to the noble race of the Atrides, he was filled with their peculiar pride and their desire for conquest. It may be also that the hope of rich booty had influenced his decision to make the whole of Troy pay for the injury and wrong done to Menelaus by Paris.

So it was that harshly he refused to grant the prayers of Chryses, the afflicted father. "Depart from me," commanded Agamemnon, "if you do not wish to arouse my anger with your vain supplication. Your daughter shall spend the rest of her days far from her own country in my palace of Argos, where she will be my handmaiden and will weave and spin."

Fearing for his life, Chryses re-embarked on his ship and besought Apollo to punish the Greeks for the wrong that they had done to him, the chosen priest of his temple. Whereupon the god, drawing his silver bow, shot forth poisoned arrows into the army of Agamemnon and spread a vile plague that caused the death of hundreds of men and horses.

"Let us take counsel together," said Achilles, "and consult the priests and seers. They will tell us why Apollo is angry with us and what sacrifice we should make to appease his wrath."

The advice of Achilles was listened to with attention,

for of all the officers in the Greek army none had more authority. His matchless valour and his splendid presence gained the admiration of them all, for was he not the son of Thetis, goddess of the waters!

So proud was he of his parentage that he only accepted Agamemnon's authority with impatience, for he considered the King to be his inferior in courage and in birth.

Calchas, the wisest of the army soothsayers, thus addressed the assembled Greeks.

"Noble Achilles and you O kings, I have just consulted the oracle of Apollo, and this is what I have discovered. The god is punishing us for having refused to return Chryseis to her father, and thus will he continue to afflict us until we return the maiden to Chryses and do not ask a ransom. . . ."

"Prophet of evil," cried Agamemnon rising up angrily from his chair. "Never have you announced a joyful event. You wish to deprive me of my captive, but never shall I consent to make this sacrifice unless others do likewise. Am I not commander of the army, and am I to be the only one to receive no booty from our victories!"

"O Agamemnon," cried Achilles, aroused to anger by this arrogance. "Well you know that the plunder has already been apportioned. When we have captured Troy, then will we give you thrice what you have lost."

"Never," cried the king of Argos in furious tones. "Never shall it be said that I, Agamemnon, would wait like a patient slave for my reward. If the Greeks will offer me nothing to make up for the loss of Chryseis. . . ."

"What then will you do?" said Achilles sharply.

Agamemnon smote on the arm of his throne with his mighty fist so that it creaked loudly.

"I will seize from you, Achilles, from Ajax or from Ulysses the prisoners that were given as your share. Chryseis must go, for the survival of the Greeks requires it, but I shall avenge myself."

"Tyrant," rejoined Achilles, exasperated with rage, "dare you take advantage of our trust in you and steal our property. You dare to threaten me, I who brought my ships and warriors to Troy to avenge the insults to your family. I have a mind to abandon you to your fate."

"What keeps you from departing?" said Agamemnon ironically. "I scorn your help. Therefore go with your men. Go! But to prove to you that it is I alone who give commands in this army, I shall take away from you Briseis, the girl who was your captive."

In a frenzy of anger, Achilles began to draw his sword, and Ulysses and Ajax swiftly placed themselves between the two kings, but as swiftly the son of Thetis mastered his anger and drove back his weapon into its sheath. Doubtless Minerva had seen that her beloved Greeks had begun to quarrel and had held back the hero's hand. Controlling himself, Achilles, looking contemptuously at Agamemnon, raised his hand heavenward to make this solemn oath:

"I swear that the day will come when my help so scornfully rejected will be sought for with desperate anxiety by the Greeks. I say to you that even if all our warriors shall be killed by the sons of Priam and by the redoubtable Hector, never will I forget the way you have insulted me."

All the Greek leaders looked at each other with the deepest concern, but such had been the anger in Achilles' voice and so fierce the resentment expressed on the faces of the two kings that no one dared to speak. Even the wily Ulysses, king of Ithaca, remained silent. Of what use was cunning and subterfuge in the presence of anger such as this? It was indeed clear that some other solution must be sought.

Therefore, when the twenty bold and energetic kings remained speechless in this quarrel which threatened to divide the Greeks, an old man rose to his feet.

It was Nestor, king of Pylos, who had brought with him to Troy no less than ninety ships. If his age prevented him from taking part in the fighting, his wise advice was listened to by everybody. Nodding his head sadly, he said in a gentle voice: "Do not let yourself be carried away by your anger, Achilles. Remember that Agamemnon became Commander by the wish of us all. His age and his high rank should make him worthy of your respect. You are the most valiant of the Greeks, Achilles, so I beg you to restrain your anger. And you, Agamemnon, though your power be great, do not act wrongfully by taking away from Achilles the slave whom he loves and whom he has received as his fair share of the spoil."

Yet did the wise Nestor speak in vain, for the bitter resentment of the kings was too great to heed advice, and the assembly separated in threatening silence. Achilles withdrew to his tent, whilst Ulysses, who had been requested by the Council to return Chryseis to her father, set off on his journey without delay.

Then did Agamemnon summon two of his officers: "Go to Achilles," he commanded, "seize Briseis and bring her to my tent. If any resistance is made to my commands, I shall know what to do."

Regretfully the officers obeyed, and when they found Achilles, the young hero was filled with sorrow and anger, yet he did nothing to prevent the departure of his beautiful captive. Achilles had sworn not to fight against the Greeks; therefore, when Briseis was led away weeping, he followed her sorrowfully with his eyes, but remained motionless.

His faithful friend, Patrocles, wished to distract him from his sorrow, but Achilles thrust him aside and began to walk along the shore murmuring the name of Briseis. Then, stretching out his arms towards the waves now gilded by the sun, he offered up a prayer to his mother, the beautiful Thetis.

The goddess had been moved by the pleas and sorrows of her son, so she hastened to him, embraced him and tried to comfort him.

"Avenge me," begged Achilles. "You have rendered great service to the king of the gods. Now plead with him on my behalf. Ask him to punish the Greeks who did not defend me, to punish the cruel and brutal Agamemnon. The Trojan warriors would not dare to stand against me. If they know that I no longer fight alongside the Greeks, they will join battle. I wish, oh, how I wish that those who have insulted Achilles could be made to wash the shore of Troy with their blood."

Thetis promised to act on his behalf and, without losing any time, she set out for Olympus.

She knelt at the feet of the king of the gods, clasped his knees and spoke humbly on behalf of her son.

"O Jupiter, ruler of the Universe, listen to my plea. Avenge my son by humiliating the Greeks and by making them feel how much they have lost by scorning the support of Achilles."

Jupiter allowed himself to be moved by the tears of this loving mother, for he knew that the career of Achilles would be a short one and that, although he might be destined to attain great and lasting glory, his life must come to an end like a flower in full bloom.

"Rise, Thetis," he said gently to the sorrowful goddess. "We will grant Achilles the satisfaction of seeing at his feet these very men who treated him without consideration. I, Jupiter, will mislead proud Agamemnon by a dream which will induce him to attempt to take Troy by storm. Thus will his army suffer great losses and thus will he learn how much it has cost him to scorn the help of a great leader such as Achilles."

Thetis rose to her feet consoled, and sped down from the heights of Olympus into her dwelling in the depths of the salty waves, but she did not forget to reassure her son, who was still wandering on the shore.

"O Patrocles," cried Achilles, running up to his friend. "Great Jupiter has heard of my sorrow, and has listened to my prayer for vengeance upon proud Agamemnon."

"Alas," sighed Patrocles. "Have you so soon forgotten that you also are a Greek and that in your anger you are condemning those who should be your brothers."

Achilles flushed when he heard these words, but his heart was still filled with anger, so he returned to his tent without saying another word. His own soldiers, the Myrmidons, obeyed his orders to pile arms and take off their bronze breastplates, but their eyes were turned longingly to the far side of the camp, where the remaining Greek warriors were training for battle. The knowledge that their brothers in arms were about to go into battle and might be victorious without their help filled these valiant soldiers with regret, but Achilles had given his orders and not one of his men dared to complain.

Now, although dawn had cast its light over the world ten times in succession, Jupiter had not forgotten his promise to Thetis, so he sent a messenger to appear in a dream to Agamemnon. He had given this phantom the features of wise Nestor and endowed him with such persuasive speech that when Agamemnon awoke he believed that this would indeed be the last day of Troy and that all the gods and goddesses were favouring the Greeks.

Leaping to his feet, he put on his purple mantle, girded on his belt and seized the ancient sceptre of his ancestors. Then, leaving his tent, he ordered the heralds to summon an assembly of his chiefs.

"Friends," he said to them, "a messenger sent by the gods visited me in a dream last night, and this is what he said: 'Jupiter is ready to support the Greeks. Summon your warriors to arms and lead them to attack, for the Trojans are threatened with destruction.' I awoke filled with such assurance that I summoned you forthwith. There can be no doubt that the gods are now on our side."

The aged Nestor nodded and, checking with a gesture the impulsive exclamations of the other leaders, he declared: "Had any other man spoken thus I might well have considered this dream to be nothing but an illusion, but it was the great Agamemnon who saw this vision and therefore it must assuredly be true. Let us arm our warriors and lead them into battle. Yet, wait. We must not forget that we have been fighting without avail for nearly ten years and our soldiers must indeed be discouraged. Therefore let us not demand this final effort, but instead let us induce them to claim the right to make it of their own accord and to fight of their own free will, inspired by true courage. So, Agamemnon, shall you test their valour, by telling them that we are about to retire and return to our own country, then assuredly will they clamour to be led into battle."

Nestor knew well the hearts of men, and Agamemnon listened to his wise advice, then summoned all the Greeks except the Myrmidons and addressed them with these words:

"Warriors, children of Hellas, Jupiter has cruelly betrayed our hopes of conquering Troy and enriching ourselves with the plunder of the city. To our shame, a people less numerous than our own has vanquished us by its resistance. We have spent nine long years in useless toil: time has destroyed our vessels and our wives and children await our return in their lonely dwellings. Since we must, let us give way to cruel necessity and regretfully return to our country, for never can Troy be ours."

A deathly silence followed this unexpected speech; each man looked upon his fellow with hesitation and uncertainty. Even Thersites, the ugliest and most cowardly of all the Greeks, who had never ceased to sow discontent in the army nor to encourage lack of respect towards his chiefs—even he remained for a moment amazed.

Before he had had time to reply to Agamemnon's speech, Ulysses rose to his feet and cried out in a loud and solemn voice. "O, King, the Greeks would not break the promise that they made you. Never will they return to Greece until proud Troy has been brought low. We have not waited so many weary years in order to depart from these shores defeated and humbled. For my part, I remember the oracles of Calchas when they told us of the promise of the king of the gods, that the throne of Priam should be destroyed by our blows. Let us not waste any more time in vain speeches. Lead us into battle, mighty Agamemnon, and may the coming of darkness alone put an end to our fighting."

A great cheer rose up from all sides, and these men who only a few minutes previously had been hesitating and perplexed could only think of one thing: the battle, the battle! For the calm courage of Ulysses had aroused their enthusiasm and increased their ardour for the fight.

Nestor upheld Ulysses in his protests and swords were brandished in a fierce call to action. Then did Agamemnon pretend to be dissuaded from his plan for retreat.

"If it is your desire to fight," he said, "let it be so. We will make this last effort. We know that the gods are on the side of the Greeks. Moved by our patience, they will assuredly reward our courage in the way that it deserves. To-morrow at dawn we shall attack. Let us make ready our arms and gain the favour of the king of the gods by offering up sacrifices to him."

All that remained of the day was given up to warlike

preparation. Slaves were busily polishing and sharpening their masters' weapons. They decorated and repaired the war chariots and mended the harnesses of the horses. The warriors were filled with enthusiasm and hope, for each of them felt assured of victory and imagined himself vanquishing some Trojan hero, perhaps even proud Hector himself. In every tent the soldiers could only speak of the booty that they hoped to gain, and the memory of the serious reverses of so many years left their minds, for they felt that Greece was indeed beloved of the gods and that this time they would surely be the victors.

2

The Results of a Duel

EAVES and flowers in the spring-time are no more numerous than were the soldiers of the Greeks on the shore of the sea and along banks of the swiftly-flowing River Scamandra.

Ajax, Ulysses, Menelaus and a hundred other captains from the mainland of Hellas and from the islands waited only for a sign from Agamemnon to leap into their war chariots.

The latter had offered up the ritual sacrifice, scattering grains of barley on the head of a five-year-old bull, which he had just killed to offer up to Jupiter.

"O mighty god," he cried, "Sovereign Lord of Olympus reigning high in the clouds, do not allow the sun to set upon these waters before the palace of Priam is in our hands and the Trojan warriors lie dying at our feet."

Even as the smoke of the burnt offering vanished in the air, the Greek commander gave the signal for departure. The chieftains sprang into their chariots, their lances and shields in their hands, whilst their tall plumes fluttered in the breeze.

Clouds of dust rose in the plain, stirred up by the trampling of thousands of feet and by the rolling of hundreds of creaking, rumbling vehicles.

Seated outside their tents near the seashore, Achilles and his warriors watched the departure of the Greek army with deep distress.

High up on the walls of Troy, the sentries were anxious and perplexed, even though the bright sun would soon flood the plain with its clear, white radiance, for did they not hear threatening sounds coming from the Greek tents dimly outlined against the far horizon? As dawn came, a mist rose, veiling everything in its soft dimness, so perhaps it was only the far-away rushing of the river that had caused their fear?

Meanwhile, Hector and Priam held a council of war in the City of Troy; one of the king's sons had climbed up to the top of a rocky height in order to observe the movements of the Greek army and had confirmed the worst fears of the sentries: the enemy host was on the march. "Let us go forthwith and attack them on the plain!" cried Hector. Seizing his helmet, he mounted his chariot and the other Trojan leaders followed his example. Trumpets pealed, summoning foot soldiers and horsemen to arms; the gates of the town were opened and the warriors poured out, following Hector closely and uttering their loud battle-cries.

Silently the Greek army advanced, and clouds of dust swirled up into the air to mark their progress.

Paris had joined his brother at the head of the Trojan army. He had thrown a leopard-skin over his glittering armour, and a sword with a fine shining hilt hung by his side. A bow and a quiverful of arrows were slung over his shoulder and in his hands he held two javelins, and from afar he began to shout out abuse at the enemy chieftains as they advanced towards him.

"Cowardly thief and seducer," roared Menelaus on seeing his hated rival. "Come and measure your might against mine, for this is the hour of vengeance!"

So threatening was the voice of the Greek King that Paris began to tremble with fear. He stepped back, trying to hide in the ranks of the Trojan warriors.

"So you would take flight," cried Hector indignantly, "you, the cause of all the difficulties that beset Ilium in our time! You who have brought upon us so many misfortunes and so much mourning."

"You have spoken truly, Hector," said Paris, turning round, crimson with shame. "How well I deserve your reproaches, but life is so sweet that he who may be about to lose it may surely falter for a moment without dishonour. Would you have me fight? If so, check the advance of both the Greeks and the Trojans, and Menelaus and I will battle against each other in the presence of both armies. Helen and her treasures shall be the reward of the victor and a treaty shall bind the two countries together: the Trojans shall remain peacefully in their own land whilst the Greeks will return to the country from which they came. Then I shall no longer be the cause of destruction and the loss of life."

Hector agreed to this suggestion and, advancing between the armies, he imposed silence with a gesture. When he made plain his brother's proposal in a loud voice, Menelaus swung down from his chariot.

"I accept this offer," he cried. "Let one of us die in battle to-day! Then shall our quarrels come to an end and mighty Priam shall come in person to conclude the treaty of peace that will follow our duel."

A joyous murmur rose up on all sides, for Trojans and Greeks believed that this long war was about to cease. Whilst the warriors grounded arms, heralds set off for Troy to invite Priam to come down into the plain.

Priam, who was seated at the gates of his city surrounded by the aged, had watched with anxious heart the young men, pride of their fatherland, set off to face the murderous perils of battle. Helen was seated at his feet, and from time to time she turned her beautiful eyes towards his majestic, gentle face. On her golden hair she had placed a veil of fine linen and a tunic over her soft white shoulders was fastened by a brooch of gold.

The eyes of them all, of the anxious, bewildered children and wise and sorrowful old men, were fixed on this woman who had brought so many misfortunes upon their country. How much blood had already been shed because of a man's love for her? What dark future would her fatal loveliness bring to them? And yet there was no murmuring, no muttered insults among these people, for she was protected by her beauty and by the love that the very sight of her aroused in all hearts. Wherever she passed there was a strange silence! Those who mourned a son, a brother or a husband, fallen because of her, turned away their heads so as not to behold her, for no one would have dared to raise a hand against this Helen, favoured by Venus, the goddess of beauty. Even Priam, the old King, extended his protection and pity to this foreign woman, whose every look seemed to plead forgiveness for having inspired so much love.

"O king," said the messengers of Hector to Priam when they arrived. "Paris and Menelaus have agreed to fight in single combat for the possession of Helen and her treasures. We would ask for your presence on the field of battle to offer up a sacrifice to the gods who created men and guide their destinies. The Trojans await you."

Helen, overwhelmed with emotion, turned towards the old man. "Daughter," said the king gently to her, "dry your tears, for, whatever shall be the outcome of this combat, you will not lack a fatherland nor a family. Oh, may the gods be content with the blood that has already flowed in this quarrel."

Whilst Helen leant sorrowfully against the battlements of the city wall, Priam climbed into his chariot and set forth at a gallop for the field of battle.

The ranks of the opposing armies faced each other in long lines across the grassy plain and the priests had brought the animals for sacrifice, as well as urns full of wine to offer up to the gods.

Agamemnon then took a knife and cut a few wisps of wool from the head of each lamb, and raised his arms heavenwards in prayer. "O father of the Immortals," he cried, "you who watch over the destinies of the Universe, mighty and terrible god, and you, O sun, eye of the world from whom nothing is hidden, you fertile earth, be witness of our oaths! Should Paris be the victor, Helen and her treasures will be his, and we shall depart for Greece. If Menelaus triumphs, let the Trojans relinquish Helen, and let Ilium remain under our domination. Listen to us, O ye gods!"

Agamemnon then plunged his knife into the flanks of each victim, and cups filled with wine were passed round to the Immortals.

As soon as the Greek commander had taken his oath, the two armies and their kings did likewise. Hector and Ulysses measured out the ground on which the combat was to take place and lots were drawn to decide which of the adversaries should strike the first blow.

So deeply was Priam moved that he could not suffer his eyes to behold the mortal combat which was about to begin. Sadly he saluted the Greeks and the Trojans and, hiding his face in his cloak, he slowly climbed into his chariot and drove back to Troy. Scarcely did the soldiers of the two armies notice his departure for their eyes were fixed upon the champions.

Each of the combatants had put on a new breastplate. The one worn by Paris shone like polished silver, and the horse's tail on the crest of his helmet floated over his shoulders, giving him a terrifying aspect. A huge shield hung on one of his arms. Less imposing though his armour might be, Menelaus was so filled with rage that his eyes were aflame, and Paris could scarcely look upon him without trembling.

Mastering his fear, the young man prepared for battle,

for the lot had fallen to him to deal the first blow. Without delaying for a moment, the young Trojan hurled his javelin forth, but it struck the shield of his opponent without piercing it, and fell to the ground with blunted point.

With a smile of triumph on his lips, Menelaus invoked the support of the king of the gods, and then sent his own shaft whistling through the air, but Paris moved swiftly aside to avoid it and thus saved himself from injury or even death.

Then the Greek seized his sword and dealt his enemy a mighty blow on the helmet, but the blade was shattered into many pieces.

"O mighty Jupiter," cried Menelaus in anguish, "why do you deal so cruelly with me? Must you indeed favour this base wretch?"

Then the Greek champion rushed towards Paris and, taking hold of the plume of his helmet, dragged him back towards his own army.

In vain did Paris try to resist, but his adversary was too strong for him and so, closing his eyes, he gave himself up to his fate.

Now the goddess Venus was watching over him and she cut the strap which held his helmet. Dismayed, Menelaus found nothing but this empty helmet grasped in his hand and in a furious rage he threw it into the midst of the Greeks. "Treason," he cried. "You hope to escape death by trickery, but this time you will not be able to ward off the blow." And he leapt back upon his enemy afresh and tried to run him through with his spear. Once more Venus was moved to intervene for her favourite, so she carried off Paris in a thick mist to hide him from the eyes of the army.

She bore him as far as Troy, to the room where Helen was sighing and weeping at her loom. "Daughter," cried the goddess. "Come. I have brought your husband, for he is weary of combat. May your love and your care make him forget the sufferings he has just endured for love of you."

Helen rose to her feet, trembling with emotion. Her thoughts had strayed far from this Asian palace and from this prince who had captured her. Instead her thoughts had turned to her former home in Sparta, to the childish laughter of the little daughter whom she had left behind in Greece and to Menelaus, the first man to win her love.

But was not Paris standing before her, smiling and holding out his hands? So, bowing her head, the beautiful Helen obeyed the wish of the goddess whom she revered and of the Prince who now possessed her.

Far away on the plain, the men of the Greek army uttered cries of triumph. "Menelaus is the victor," they cried. "Paris has fled and the Trojans give him shelter in their ranks. The beautiful Helen herself belongs to us as well as the treasures which she brought away from Sparta. Now shall Ilium be under the sway of Hellas!"

Then did the Greek chiefs surround Menelaus and applaud him, whilst Hector and the Trojans stood by, petrified with astonishment. They could not understand how Paris had disappeared. "What has become of our champion?" they asked themselves. "The gods," murmured some with frightened glances, for it seemed to them that there must have been divine intervention and they trembled in awe. Hector, pale as a ghost, listened without understanding the loud cries of joy and pride which resounded throughout the ranks of the opposing army.

Yet he had sworn to respect the outcome of the duel, whatever it might be. So his hand rested on the hilt of his sword to throw it at the feet of the conqueror. In the meantime, whilst tumult and confusion prevailed among men, the gods, seated at their festive table, joyously toasted each other with their golden cups full of nectar as they watched the happenings on the plain of Troy. Jupiter had perceived the trick by which Venus had saved Paris. Juno and Minerva had also been witness to it and had become angry, but the king of the gods silenced their protests with a gesture.

"Minerva," he said, in command, "the Trojans cannot escape their fate, and although my heart is filled with sorrow at the thought, Ilium shall not survive to be a peaceful and prosperous colony, but must indeed be reduced to a heap of ruins as the Fates decreed. In years to come all that the passer-by shall see there will be mounds of grass-grown earth. Go! Fill the minds of these men who are disposed to keep their word with the most bitter thoughts of resistance and vengeance."

Scarcely had Jupiter spoken than Minerva glided down upon earth like a golden and fiery star. Her flight through the heavens filled the two armies with awe and astonishment, but already the goddess of war had approached Pandarus, doughtiest of Trojan leaders, and had whispered these words in his ear.

"Brave warrior, are you prepared to accept defeat so

easily after so many years of courageous resistance? Direct your sharpest arrow at this overbearing Menelaus. You will strike him down without difficulty, for he is unprepared, and thus will you have earned the praise of your country and all its allies by killing this man, the source of all the woes of Ilium."

Now, Pandarus was indeed sorrowful at the thought of seeing Greece triumphing over Troy, so this secret voice which encouraged him to continue the struggle filled him with joy.

"Hide me behind your shields," he asked his companions, "that I may flex my bow, and then may the god Apollo guide my arrows straight into the heart of our bitter foe!" So saying, he bent down and, picking out from his quiver a well-feathered shaft, he drew his bowstring just as Minerva rushed forward and turned aside the missile with her hand. Thus, instead of striking Menelaus in the chest, at the joint of his breastplate, the arrow wounded him in the side after striking the buckle of his belt.

Even so, his blood began to flow and, as Menelaus staggered, his brother Agamemnon seized his hand saying in a sorrowing voice: "Alas, O Menelaus, the Trojans were plotting your death. Whether you had conquered or been conquered in this duel, they had decided upon your doom. Be assured that we will avenge your defeat. Their lives and those of their wives and children shall pay dearly for this treachery. Tell me! do you suffer great pain and is your wound mortal?"

·"Be calm," replied Menelaus in a firm voice. "Do not spread alarm among our soldiers, but send for a surgeon to dress my injuries."

Without delay, Agamemnon ordered Menelaus to be carried from the field of battle and, after having pulled the arrow out of his flesh, Machaon, the surgeon, applied all the skilful remedies he had learnt from the centaur Chiron. Then the Greeks prepared for battle.

Agamemnon walked up and down the ranks to stir the courage of his men, but he had no need to do so, for the Greeks were already filled with indignation and rage against the Trojans, who had so basely broken faith. Each one was determined to avenge the King whom they honoured for his bravery.

Accordingly, Ajax, Ulysses, the aged Nestor and all the other chieftains assembled their troops. They marched forward in a terrible and threatening silence with their weapons shining like waves driven by the wind against the rock until they are covered with snow-white foam.

On the Trojan side there was loud clamour, for they had seen Menelaus fall and they believed that he was dead. So deeply were they moved by this tragedy that not only were they prepared to resist the onslaught of the Greeks, but were even ready to attack in their turn. For a while Hector had hesitated, but his country was dearer to him than his plighted word to an enemy, and he set off at the head of his army.

Now the gods took sides in this mighty struggle between mortals. Mars upheld the Trojans, and Minerva favoured the Greeks. Fierce battle was joined by these warring hosts, arousing cries of pain and anger and spreading death and carnage on all sides.

Helmets, shields and swords clashed with fearful tumult amidst confusion, slaughter, shouts of pain and shouts of triumph. Antilochus, son of Nestor, plunged his sword into the chest of Echepolus, the Trojan, who fell to the ground moaning in anguish. Elephenor rushed forward to seize the armour of a dying foe, but Agenor prevented him from doing so by stabbing him in the flank. Trojans and Greeks fought over the spoils of the fallen.

The handsome Simoisius rolled to the ground in a death agony, pierced through and through by the lance of Ajax. Hardly had he done so than Leucus, a companion of Ulysses, fell on the top of him. The Trojans began to withdraw, dragging back Hector in their retreat, whilst the Greeks rushed forward in pursuit, uttering loud cries of triumph.

Minerva was in their midst encouraging those whom she saw were ready to retreat, but as Apollo had joined Mars to give help to the Trojans, the fighting became more bitter and men fell in greater numbers. The Aetolian, Thoas, had turned his javelin against the Trojan Piros, whose companions pressed around him to protect him with their swords, but soon the two opposing chieftains were lying in the dust surrounded by their wounded and dead supporters.

The valiant Diomedes was ever in the thickest of the battle, with his shield and helmet throwing off sparks like an anvil. He had leapt down from his chariot to fight more nimbly and the Trojans tried to hem him in on all sides. Two of their number paid with their lives for their boldness in attacking the Greek hero. Javelins flew through the air in all directions; blood flowed in streams. Even the gods could not watch such a spectacle unmoved, and Minerva became weary of the slaughter and took Mars by the hand.

"God of Battle," she said quickly, "is it necessary that you should intervene between these men caught up in this terrible slaughter? This is surely not a task for immortals? Let us depart, let us leave Greeks and Trojans to the fight and let us return to our Olympian heights, where peace and eternal joy await us." Whereupon Mars pretended to obey and the two gods flew away, turning aside from this field of slaughter, where death was ever hovering and mowing down these men of noble courage. Agamemnon, who was leading the Greek army, forced the Trojans to give way before his onslaught, but Diomedes' exploits were rivalling his own and stimulating him to greater valour.

Suddenly the latter uttered a cry: an arrow had pierced the joint in his armour and penetrated deep into his shoulder. He staggered as a mist rose up before his eyes.

"Sthenelus," demanded Diomedes of his squire, who ran up trembling at the sight of so great a flow of blood, "pull out this shaft which is rending my flesh. Do not shudder for I am sustained by the idea of vengeance. Never will I die before chastising the bold man who has wounded me." And, raising up his eyes to heaven he prayed: "O Minerva, O daughter of Jupiter, I beg only one favour, deliver up to my blows the warrior who has wounded me and who believes that he is killing me."

Now Minerva paid heed to the fierce prayer of the hero, and soon Pandarus appeared before his eyes, for it was he who had let fly the deadly arrow. Believing that his opponent was more seriously wounded than was the case, the Trojan rushed forward fearlessly, so that he might deal the fatal blow and carry off his weapons as booty.

On seeing what was happening, Diomedes forgot his wound and, sword in hand, he leapt towards the Trojan. Two of his comrades tried in vain to prevent the onslaught of the Greek; two more attempted to overthrow him with their chariot wheels, but nothing could stem the furious advance of Diomedes.

"Vile Greek," cried Pandarus, who had climbed up into the chariot of his friend Aeneas, "since my arrows did not put an end to your life, let us see if my javelins will fare better." His missile flew through the air and, piercing the shield of Diomedes, struck his breastplate.

"Your shafts only serve to revive the drooping spirits of the weak," scoffed the hero. "Now you may say farewell to this world."

The Greek's javelin sped fast through the air and struck Pandarus in the face, killing him instantly, but his friend Aeneas, wishing to protect the corpse from desecration, covered it with his own body and his shield. A second javelin, thrown by Diomedes, penetrated his thigh, but immediately his comrades seized the wounded man, and bore him swiftly away from the battlefield.

Then began a confused struggle around the dead body of Pandarus and the chariot of Aeneas, whose horses began to whinny with terror. Agamemnon, Menelaus— who was already recovering from his injury—and several other Greek champions ran up to join Diomedes, and made a great effort to scatter the enemy ranks and transform their retreat into a rout.

But soon the Greeks began to give way in their turn,

and Diomedes grew chill with fear, for in front of him, and in front of his men, who were already buoyed up with thoughts of victory, stood Hector.

The Trojan champion had struck down two of the boldest of his foes with his javelins, launched with unerring aim. Since the Greeks could not stand up to this human whirlwind, they began to give way, but they still fought on courageously, even though Hector ploughed through the ranks of his enemies, killing many of the bravest and doughtiest of their number.

When she saw how many of her beloved Greeks had succumbed in this sternest of battles, Juno began to tremble over the fate of those that remained. Whereupon she summoned Minerva. "Daughter of Jupiter," she cried, "we promised Menelaus that he would be able to destroy Troy and return as conqueror to the land of his fathers. Is it right that we should leave him defenceless against Hector? Let us harness war-horses to my chariot of gold and bronze. Put on your breastplate and take up your shield and the lance that has caused the death of so many heroes. As for you, O Jupiter, can you not give me leave to punish Mars for the favour that he is showing the Trojans! In spite of our agreement, he has returned to the dread field of battle and, walking before Hector, he is helping to spread death and destruction among the ranks of the Hellenes."

Jupiter gave his assent and the two goddesses lost no time in descending among the Greeks. Soon Juno, driving her own swift horses, arrived in the place where the battle was being waged most fiercely and, as she advanced, she encountered Greeks who were fleeing ever faster. In order to make herself acceptable in their eyes, she took on the features and body of one of the boldest of their leaders whose voice carried very far.

"Cowards," she cried out to the fugitives. "What kind of warriors are you? Would you have the Trojans believe that Achilles alone is capable of standing firm? Whither are you flying. Are you going to allow your enemies to follow you and slaughter you on your own ships?"

These words aroused all her listeners, and the Greeks began to gather round their heroic leaders, Agamemnon, Menelaus and Diomedes, who were retreating slowly, defending every foot of the ground before yielding. Diomedes, still bleeding and exhausted, continued to fight from his chariot.

Much relieved at the renewed resistance and courage of her friends the Greeks, Juno became invisible once more and flew up to Mars, ordering him in the name of the king of the gods to lay down his arms.

Now, Mars did not dare to disobey the commands of Jupiter, so, with hanging head and filled with sadness at having to desert his beloved Trojans at such a time, he followed the goddesses back to the peace of Olympus, to take his seat at the banquet of endless festivities.

Far below, beneath the layer of cloud stirred up by the fighting, men still struggled and killed each other on the dusty field of battle, inspired as ever by their hatred and their thirst for vengeance.

So it was that dead bodies continued to drift down the blood-stained waters of the rivers Zanthe and Simois.

Ajax and Diomedes vied with each other in prowess, and their foes fell around them like ripe ears of wheat heaped in the fields under the warm sun. Their squires stripped the dead Trojans of their armour and piled up the trophies in the chariots of their chiefs.

For a long while Menelaus had been pursuing a Trojan leader named Adreastes, and finally he held him at his mercy when one of his horses shied and threw him to the ground.

"Spare me," said the Trojan, clasping the knees of his conqueror. "Only grant me my life and all the treasures of my father's palace will be yours. Have mercy!"

Menelaus, moved by this supplication, called his squire and bade him take the captive back to his ship, but Agamemnon approached and cried out in fury: "Unfortunate man, what are you about to do? Not a single Trojan shall escape alive from our hands. We have sworn it. Have you no fear that the gods will make you pay dearly for this moment of weakness?" And, with a mighty stroke of his sword, Agamemnon killed the Trojan. All around them arose the cries of the dying that echoed across the wide and melancholy plain.

3

Hector's Farewell

OWN in the Temple of Minerva there was praying and supplication: the women of Troy were imploring the goddess to help them in their distress. They brought her a veil woven in threads of gold and purple, which they placed upon her knees. Then, with loud cries of distress, they raised up their hands towards the statue of the great Minerva: "O protectress of our walls," they said to her, "take pity on us; disarm the Greeks, and abase Diomedes, and we will sacrifice to you twelve of the finest heifers every year. Be favourable to us, we implore you. . . ."

Whilst these vain prayers were being offered up to the relentless goddess, Hector had returned to the city. There he sought out Paris, whom he had not seen on the field of battle since the coward had fled in the middle of his duel with Menelaus. As the hero entered his brother's palace, he looked scornfully at the extravagant luxury of this dwelling, where gold and silver gleamed in every room.

"Where are you, Paris?" shouted Hector, striding through the palace. "Where have you been hiding whilst we have been fighting your battle, and whilst the soil of our plains is steeped in Trojan blood? Can you allow Troy to be destroyed without attempting to do your part in defending our fatherland?"

Paris stood before him, pale and filled with shame. "It is true that I deserve your reproaches, brother," he admitted, "but, see, I was preparing to go out to battle again, I was polishing my armour and making ready my bow. I will join you on the ramparts without delay."

Hector did not deign to reply to his brother, but he turned towards Helen, who was now approaching him, and said, "Sister, see to it that Paris does not take too long before coming to share the dangers that we have to face in defence of our city. No," he added, seeing that the young woman was about to bring him some food. "I cannot rest so long as the Trojans have need of me, and I wish to embrace my wife, Andromache, and my small son. Alas, perhaps I shall never see them again, for doubtless the gods have decreed that I shall die."

"Brother," she said timidly, "I beg you to take a sip of this wine. Assuredly your weariness has made you thirsty. Forgive, I pray you, the misfortunes and the dangers which I have unwittingly caused. I would that Paris alone could endure with me the whole force of the calamity for which he is responsible! But you must surely know that he can only display courage when he is with women and with slaves."

Then Helen and Hector looked contemptuously at Paris. "Lose no time in joining us," said Hector harshly. "Our fate is in the balance, our soldiers are worn out, and it is we who must set them a good example."

Hector then left the palace, for he was burning with the desire to see his family. "Where is Andromache?" he cried to his old nurse, who knelt before him weeping. "Is she here or is she praying in the Temple of Minerva with the other Trojan women?"

"She is on the ramparts with your son, for there was a rumour that the Greeks were triumphing."

But Hector was no longer listening, for he had set off at full speed to find his much-loved wife. Soon he perceived Andromache leaning over the battlements, scanning feverishly the field of battle to try to discover what had happened to her husband's chariot. Next to her stood the nurse, with the baby, Astyanax, in her arms, waving his hands and laughing at all the strange noises that he heard rising from below.

Hector paused a moment to take in this sad little group: the young woman with her face strained by anxiety, the little child, whose joyous heedlessness stressed the poignant concern and perplexity of his mother. Andromache turned round and with a cry of delirious relief she embraced her husband, stroking his rough armour, resting her head on his shoulder and weeping.

"Hector," she said, "madness has seized you. Stay

here, I beseech you, for what good can come of these battles in the plain far from our strong ramparts? Remain here in this mighty tower, for your presence is needed, I do assure you. More than once have the Greeks attempted to break through at this point, for they must know that this is the weakest place in our defences. Beloved husband, do you not understand that without leaving Troy you may be able to defend her more valiantly?"

Hector smiled at this advice, and embraced his wife again. "War is not so simple as that," he replied, "and if leaders and princes did not set an example and were not the first to face the greatest dangers, they would have cause for real shame. Do not believe that my thoughts are far from you even in those terrible moments when men are being killed all around me. Dear Andromache, if I continue this struggle, it is less for the glory of my father, the safety of his kingdom and the lives of all the Trojans, than because of you and of our son. Sometimes I see you before my eyes, a slave overcome with sorrow and despair, drawing water and spinning for some other woman. In my imagination I can hear the Greeks saying to each other ironically: 'There goes the wife of Hector, the famous warrior who commanded the Trojans when we fought beneath the walls of Ilium.' What a vile image! I would rather be buried in the tomb than see you struggling in the grasp of a bloodthirsty foe who is trying to drag you away."

"Should I survive you," declared Andromache, "I would have you know that I shall spend all my days and nights in mourning." For a moment they stood close together, thinking on the dark future that lay before them, for they were filled with the same dread forebodings. As Hector turned towards his son, wishing to clasp him once more in his arms, the child began to weep and clung to his nurse, frightened by the warrior's big helmet and the tall plumes in its crest.

"Poor child," said Andromache, smiling through her tears. "He also senses that he is going to lose you."

Hector placed his helmet on the ground and, taking the infant in his arms, looked at him with great tenderness. "O ye gods, make my son follow in my footsteps. That when he returns to these same ramparts, laden with spoils and booty, men may say: 'He is even braver than his father.'" Handing back the baby to his wife, he pressed them both lovingly in his arms and then prepared to depart. "Dear wife," said Hector steadying his voice, "no man can escape his destiny. Go back to the palace. I must do my duty."

And whilst Andromache watched him stride away with sorrow in her heart, the old men and women looked sadly at Hector, for they too knew that he would never return to them.

As he reached the gate of the city he felt a hand on his shoulder. It was Paris, who had rejoined him as he had promised, fully armed and laughing confidently. Hector was now reassured and ready to forgive the past misdeeds of his brother and to forget the cowardice that had caused the Trojans to sneer.

"Come," said Hector, taking his hand. "Let us conquer or die together," and they both hastened towards the plain.

" O ye gods, make my son follow in my footsteps"

On seeing them, the Trojans, who were by now worn out with the stress of battle, felt courage and hope return. Almost at once Hector and Paris killed two of the doughtiest Greek champions, and the battle raged more furiously than ever. From the heights of Olympus the gods watched the struggle, and their hearts were wrung with sorrow at seeing so many brave men die. With one accord, they decided to induce men to find some other means of settling their bloodthirsty quarrels. They selected Helenus, one of the fifty sons of Priam, to be their messenger and explain their plan. The latter went to Hector and persuaded him to separate the Greeks from the Trojans by challenging the bravest of his enemies to single combat.

Hector agreed to do so and, stepping out between the two armies, he shouted in a loud voice: "Give heed to my words, O Greeks. There are certainly great and courageous champions in your ranks. Which of them is ready to fight with me as man to man? If I fall, my arms will belong to the victor. If I win, I will take his as my rightful spoils, but our bodies must be handed back to our own people so that they may receive the full burial deserved of heroes. Which of you is prepared to take up my challenge?"

The Greek leaders looked at each other with hesitation, for Hector's prowess was famed throughout the land. "Is there no one ready to be our champion?" murmured Nestor sorrowfully.

Then Menelaus rose to his feet and declared "If no one else is prepared to face Hector, I will do so." Immediately nine other chiefs rushed forward, including

Agamemnon, Diomedes, Ulysses and Ajax, all of them vying with each other for the honour of fighting Hector. "Now must they draw lots," said the wise Nestor; "and may Jupiter favour Ajax or Diomedes." This advice was followed, and the Fates decreed that Ajax should be the champion of the Greeks. Filled with pride and joy at this great honour, Ajax rushed out to encounter Hector, whilst his fellow Greeks besought Jupiter to grant him victory.

Immediately the two heroes began to taunt each other.

"Do not try to frighten me like a child," cried Hector, "for I am well versed in warfare."

"Come and learn how the Greeks deal with those who try and scorn them," shouted Ajax, advancing. "We have a thousand champions worthy of your valour."

Hector struck first, throwing his javelin with all his strength, but it did not pierce the shield of his adversary. Then Ajax flung his shaft, and though it struck his opponent, it did not succeed in penetrating his breast-plate.

"Close in," cried Hector, running forward and lunging out with his spear, but the blow was warded off. Ajax, in his turn, thrust right through the Trojan's shield. Slightly wounded in the throat, Hector staggered, but did not give up the combat and, seizing an enormous stone, he balanced it over his head and slung it against his enemy's buckler.

Then Ajax unsheathed his sword, whilst Hector did likewise, and at once they came together in deadly strife. Indeed, it seemed as if they might kill each other, and so once again the gods relented and extended the sceptre of peace over the combatants. "Night has fallen," they said, "you must respect the powers of darkness and cease fighting." Ajax turned towards Hector to show that the decision to end their duel lay with him. Hector held out his hand to him.

"Let us obey the voice of the gods," he said gravely. "We will take up arms again another day and fight to the death. Accept as a token of my respect this sword and this golden belt so that those who witnessed our contest may say: 'They fought with fury, but they parted friends.'"

Having made a similar gift to his opponent, Ajax withdrew to Agamemnon's tent and, later, after having sacrificed a heifer to Jupiter, he took part in the great feast, which all the Greek leaders attended.

Whilst they were seated at table, they decided that the next day should be given up to collecting the dead and burying them with due ceremony. As well as this, they determined to build a great wall with towers and gates and a deep ditch to protect their encampment and their ships. At dawn, as they were about to separate, they were informed that heralds had arrived from Troy.

"O Greeks," said the leader of this mission, "lend me your ears. Priam and the Trojans have asked me to put forward proposals for peace. All the treasures that Paris took away from Greece are to be returned to you with many others besides, but we are to keep Helen."

"You will keep her only until the day when we shall come to fetch her from the burning city of Troy," cried Diomedes angrily, "and that day is near, for I can feel it in my bones. Why else should you come to us offering these terms? As for the treasures, we do not need them."

All the Greek leaders applauded this speech, and Agamemnon added: "You have heard our reply, herald, and so you have an answer for the Trojans. Tell them, besides, that if they will have it so, we will spend this day paying a last tribute to our dead. . . ."

All day long, the men of the two nations worked at their task and, after the last flames of the funeral pyres had died down in the dense darkness of the night, they returned to their quarters, the Greeks to their ships, the Trojans to the ramparts of the city.

The next morning Agamemnon and his soldiers were astir even before the sun had spread its golden light on the fields and the mountain-tops. All that day, and all through the next night they toiled to build fortifications around their camp. When at last they saw the fiery light of dawn tingeing the sky with red, the Greeks believed that this day would witness their final, decisive victory.

They were mistaken. Seated on Mount Ida with his scales in his hands, Jupiter had weighed the fate of the Trojans against that of their adversaries from Hellas, but the balance was against the Greeks. So, in spite of their bravery and the suffering of their chiefs, by the time the radiant sun had set, many more Greeks had seen it for the last time.

So the battle began again, and was waged more fiercely and with greater courage than ever; men seemed to have aroused themselves only to kill each other in greater numbers.

Jupiter sighed and turned his eyes away sorrowfully

from this spectacle, and then he made his thunders roar. On this day, destined to be so fatal to the Greeks, he threw down upon them the thunderbolts and the lightning that he bore in his hands.

On the plain, the horses reared up and shied; they stampeded in all directions, heedless of the men who tried to control them. Then would chariots collide against each other, and when Nestor's was overturned the old King would have been in dire peril had not Diomedes speeded to his rescue.

"O venerable Nestor," he said, reining in his horses and offering his hand to the old man, "climb into my chariot beside me. You shall drive whilst I undertake the fighting and follow my desire to attack Hector. Should Jupiter decree our downfall and destruction to-day, I shall not go down into the Kingdom of the Dead without fighting."

Nestor climbed in next to the hero and, goad in hand, he steered the chariot towards Hector's. Diomedes then threw his javelins into the ranks of the Trojans and made many a gap in their line, but suddenly a thunderbolt fell at the feet of his horses. Neighing loudly and mad with terror, they reared up on their hind legs.

"Use your goad, wise Nestor," cried Diomedes, preparing to throw another javelin. "No, Diomedes," said the old King of Pylos. "You are wrong, We must retreat. This thunderbolt is a proof that Jupiter is fighting against us, and there is not a mortal who can strive against his supreme will. Who knows if the victory which he is granting to-day to our enemies will not perhaps be given to us to-morrow."

Tears of rage flowed from the eyes of Diomedes. To run away from Hector! What shame and despair! But wise Nestor had spoken, and he could not fail to follow his advice. This time the chariot speeded towards the Greek ships, closely followed by the terrified foot-soldiers. It was no mere retreat; it was a panic-stricken rout. Nestor was broken-hearted. Three times, when Diomedes beseeched him to do so, did he try to make his horses wheel round, to turn them against the enemy, who was advancing triumphantly, but three times were they checked by a thunderbolt. So, without resisting Jupiter's wrath any longer, the Greeks ran to seek refuge behind those walls which the wisdom and prudence of Agamemnon had made them build the day before.

Hector was triumphant, and, throwing his javelins into the thick of the fugitives, he killed many of their number. Loudly, he urged on his horses. "Speed on! Speed on!" he cried, "so that, thanks to your fleetness, I may catch up bold Diomedes and tear from him the breast-plate that the god Vulcan forged for him. This very night we shall force the Greeks back on to their ships."

Encouraged by Hector, the Trojans rushed forward. The Greeks streamed on like frightened sheep driven by a storm towards their stables, but at last, near their ships, they rallied. Yet to what purpose, for in vain they besought the help of the gods, who were powerless. Jupiter had spoken, and dread would be the punishment of any divinity bold enough to defy him. With bitter sorrow, Juno and Minerva watched from the heights of Olympus the slaughter of the army which they loved so dearly. But he who commands both gods and men and binds the strongest wills intervened. Night was now spreading her black veils over the field of battle and of death, hindering the movements of both victor and vanquished.

"Warriors," cried Hector to the Trojans, climbing out of his chariot, and assembling his chiefs around him, "I had hoped that this day would see the destruction of the Greeks and of their vessels, that we should have returned to Troy in triumph, but the darkness hides our enemies from us. We must now rest so as to regain our strength, but I shall see to it that the Greeks do not try to sail away whilst we are sleeping. Let fires be kindled and kept burning until the coming of dawn. Let supplies be brought out from Troy, and we must see to it that the women, the children and the old keep watch on the battlements so that the city may not be taken unawares by the enemy in our absence.

"We must, indeed, be on our guard throughout the night, Trojans; to-morrow at dawn we will bring death and destruction to the Greek fleet. I have a premonition that to-morrow will be a fatal day for our foes."

Filled with hope once more, the Trojans forgot their weariness and their sufferings; they unharnessed their horses, still dripping with sweat and covered with dust. Cattle and sheep, wheat and wine were brought out from Troy, and the leaping flames of the camp-fires lit up the plain as far as the shore where the Greek ships were at anchor. In spite of their fatigue, many of the warriors remained awake, for they were awaiting the appearance of dawn with impatience.

Whilst the Trojans were busying themselves in this

way, the Greeks remained near their ships, worn out and overcome with despair. In the meantime, Agamemnon summoned his chieftains to a council of war, and addressed them thus:

"Comrades," he faltered in a broken voice, "Jupiter has deceived us by promises of victory through the mouths of the oracles. Defeated and dishonoured, I must lead back to Greece the survivors of our once-powerful army. Troy is invincible, for Jupiter protects her."

In the mournful silence that followed these despairing words, a harsh, loud voice resounded suddenly. Diomedes had risen to his feet.

"Agamemnon," he said, "I pray you forgive my boldness, but I cannot remain silent after hearing your cowardly advice. Is flight the only remedy for our present plight? Is it for this kind of leadership that we chose you as our Commander? Go, if you wish. I will stay behind and remain here until Troy surrenders. The gods guided us to these shores and they must grant us victory."

A loud cheer greeted these brave words. Nestor came up and shook Diomedes by the hand. "O bravest of the brave," he said, "you are also the wisest among us all. Agamemnon is our King. His discouragement will not last, and assuredly his courage will return. Since we are worn out with fatigue, let us rest whilst the youngest and strongest of our warriors keep watch on our walls. As for us, we must ponder over the fact that to-morrow will bring us glory or shame, victory or defeat." Nestor paused a moment, but all had listened to him respectfully.

"Agamemnon," he continued, "did I not warn you against taking away Briseis from Achilles, for I foresaw that the discord would bring calamity to us all. Were Achilles with us now, accompanied by his brave men, Hector would not dare to venture so close to our camp. Why should we not try to calm the anger and resentment of the bravest of our champions?"

"True," cried all the chieftains in unison. "If Achilles were with us now, taking part in our councils and fighting at our side, we should be victorious once more."

"Wisely spoken, Nestor," agreed Agamemnon sadly. "I was blind and overbearing and did not appreciate Achilles' worth. Now I would wish to make him forget our quarrel. First of all, I will return Briseis to him, and with her I will also send captives and twelve splendid horses that have raced many a time to victory, besides ten talents of gold and many other treasures. When Troy falls, then shall he take all the gold and silver he covets and twenty of the most beautiful Trojan girls. Lastly, if ever I return to Argos, I will give him the hand of one of my three daughters in marriage and he shall receive from me seven powerful cities."

"Mighty Agamemnon, you have indeed spoken well," said Nestor, nodding his white head. "Let us choose ambassadors well liked by him. Ulysses and Ajax are his close friends. Let them set off at once, taking with them Phoenix, whom he honours for his wisdom. Friends, depart with all speed, and do not forget that all the hopes of Greece are in your hands."

Confidence returned to the hearts of all his listeners as the three envoys set off on their mission. When they came near to the tent occupied by Achilles, sounds of music reached their ears. Achilles was singing of the deeds of great heroes to the strains of his lyre. This was the manner in which he consoled himself for his inaction. Near to him sat his friend, Patrocles, listening, but also trying to hear the noise from his countrymen's encampment.

On seeing the three envoys, Achilles put aside his lyre and greeted them with outstretched arms. "Friends," he declared, "the dearest of my comrades are ever welcome here," and he ordered fruit, meat and wine to be brought to them.

When their cups had been filled, Ulysses began to explain his mission:

"Achilles," he said gravely, "we tremble for the safety of Greece. Without the help of your courage and valour, I fear that our fate is sealed. The Trojans are encamped near our walls and the light of their fires even reaches our tents. Hector is only waiting for the day to dawn to swoop down on us. He intends to set fire to our ships and bury us in their ashes. Now, Agamemnon offers you presents worthy of your rank and fame. Not only will he return Briseis, but he will also give you seven slaves, twelve horses . . ."

And the wily Ulysses continued to enumerate the gifts that were to be offered and to stress their immense value. "Achilles," he added, seeing that the hero listened to him with disdain, "if these presents are no inducement to you, you may perhaps show pity for the plight of Greece and grant us the help of your mighty arm."

"Ulysses," replied Achilles coldly. "I will speak plainly. I stormed more than twenty cities, I brought

Agamemnon vast treasures, yet he has rewarded everyone but me. The only way he repaid me was by taking away Briseis. Now the whole of Greece took up arms because of Helen, and we all made the cause of Menelaus our own. Why then should he alone be helped to take vengeance for the wrong done to him? I loved Briseis. Agamemnon took her from me, so I am revenging myself. To-morrow will I sail back to Greece with all my ships, and within the space of three days, if I am favoured, I shall sight the shores of Thessaly. I do not hate Hector. Then why should I fight against him? What does all the wealth of Troy mean to me? Indeed, I value my life more highly. Did not my mother say to me in the years gone by: 'If ever you go to Troy you will surely die there.' I have no wish to join the immortals, for life will assuredly bring me many delights. That is my reply to all your offers, and to this I would add one piece of advice. 'Flee from these shores before it is too late, for Troy will never be yours.'"

When he had finished speaking, Phoenix approached him, with tears in his eyes. "Achilles," he said, "do not be so relentless, for even the gods allow themselves to be persuaded by the prayers of those who weep. See my tears, and do not abandon Greece when she is threatened with defeat and destruction. If you spurn our demands and our gifts to-day, even should you be seized with remorse and decide to return to us later, we shall feel no gratitude."

"What does the gratitude of the Greeks mean to me?" said Achilles harshly. "The Greeks have offended me, but you, my dear Phoenix, you are my friend. Stay with me, whilst Ajax and Ulysses bear the message of my refusal to Agamemnon."

"Achilles," murmured Ajax, deeply hurt, "are you without pity? Does our friendship mean nothing to you? Can you never forgive?"

Achilles bowed his head, but he did not dare obey the impulses of his heart. Then once again he felt his resentment well up within him.

"Never," he repeated angrily. "I shall only take up arms when I see Hector slaughtering my own men in our camp, and setting our ships alight. Then I shall know how to stop him and how to defeat him."

Ulysses and Ajax departed and, sighing and full of regret, they joined Agamemnon in his tent where all the Greek leaders were holding a council.

"Tell me," asked Agamemnon anxiously, "does he still persist in his attitude?"

"Yes," replied Ulysses; "he rejects our prayers and your gifts. To-morrow his fleet will leave these shores. Moreover, he advised us to cease from besieging this city, which is clearly under the protection of Jupiter. Achilles also added that never would he fight until the day when Hector begins to slaughter his Myrmidons in their own tents. That is his full reply."

Overwhelmed with sorrow, all the Greeks remained silent. Diomedes alone stood up. "Agamemnon," he said "you were wrong to make these offers to Achilles. The prospect of these gifts made this proud, haughty man still prouder. So let us trouble no more about him. Whether he goes or whether he stays is nothing to us. A few hours remain to us before the dawn. Let us spend them in sleep, so that when the sun begins to lighten the land, we shall have renewed our strength for the conflict. Then will you muster your men, and instil into them the will to fight by the inspiration of your heartening encouragement."

4

The Battle Continues

 UCH disturbed in mind and spirit, Agamemnon was unable to find rest in sleep. "O gods," he sighed, "what will happen to us to-morrow? Assuredly Jupiter has abandoned us and the Greek army is threatened with destruction and disgrace. What grief to think that I may be vanquished by these barbarians!"

Leaping up from his couch, since he could no longer endure the peaceful shelter of his tent, he went out and cast his eyes over the plain: with fear in his heart, he saw the lights of thousands of camp-fires; the threatening cries of the enemy and the clash of arms reached his ears.

"How unfortunate we are!" he murmured, pressing his hand against his brow. "The Trojans are not sleeping. They may be about to take advantage of the darkness to creep up and slaughter our exhausted warriors. What is to be done? Whom am I to consult? Since I am undecided, I must seek some wise advice."

Putting on his tunic and his sandals and casting a lion-skin over his shoulders, he took up a javelin and walked a few steps away from his tent, and then advanced with care so as not to tread on the outstretched bodies of his sleeping soldiers. Suddenly he started as a hand touched his own.

"Is that you, brother?" said the voice of Menelaus. "Why do you go forth armed in this way? Let one of us go and try to discover the enemies' plans, but it is unwise for you to venture out by yourself in this darkness."

"Are you not able to sleep?" interrupted Agamemnon sadly.

"How could I possibly do so?" sighed Menelaus. "I feel responsible for the death of so many brave Greeks, and I think with horror that because of me thousands more will be killed and buried in this foreign soil. It seems as if we shall all be destroyed by the attacks of the invincible Hector."

"It is only by keeping calm and displaying courage that we can survive and perhaps even conquer," replied Agamemnon. "I am going to seek the advice of wise old Nestor. As for you, rouse our warriors and try to encourage them." A few moments later Agamemnon wakened Nestor, and together they went to speak to Ulysses in his tent.

"Are we being attacked?" asked the latter.

"No," replied Nestor quickly; "but we are still debating what to do. Let us find Ajax, Diomedes and the valiant Meges, and together we will decide what we should do to save the honour of Greece."

Shortly afterwards they were joined by Diomedes and several other chieftains and together they hastened to the walls of the camp.

"Friends," said Nestor, "One of us must make his way into the camp of the Trojans so that we may discover their plans."

"Nestor," replied Diomedes, "if Ulysses is prepared to go with me on this dangerous mission, I will accompany him."

The two chiefs got up hastily, watched by all their comrades, who were envious of the great honour that they had taken upon themselves. They helped them to test out the equipment that they were to take with them. One gave his sword to Diomedes, who had left his own behind in his tent. Another placed on the head of Ulysses his leather helmet surmounted by the horns of an ox, and then the two heroes went out into the darkness.

They had scarcely walked a few paces when Ulysses suddenly grasped Diomedes by the arm: a heron was flying towards them. "Will he pass to the left or to the right of us?" he said anxiously. "Can it be that the gods are on our side? O Minerva," he added fervently, turning his eyes up to the starry sky. "Deign to protect our efforts, and our gratitude will be eternal. Listen to our prayers, mighty goddess!"

In her dwelling in cloud-capped Olympus, Minerva must have heard the supplication of this King, whom she loved above all others, for the heron flew to the right of the two warriors. Since this was considered to be a sign of

future great good fortune, both Ulysses and Diomedes
continued on their way with renewed determination and
courage.

Time passed slowly, as their advance in the darkness
was far from easy, for at every step they stumbled over
dead bodies or weapons cast aside by soldiers as they fell
beneath the blows of their enemies.

A faint noise, growing ever louder, reached their ears
and soon they could discern faintly the outline of a man
advancing towards them from the Trojan camp.

"Listen," said Ulysses to Diomedes in a whisper.
"Hector must have had the same idea as we have had,
and he has despatched one of his soldiers to discover our
plans, unless by chance this may be a scavenger who is
plundering the dead in the dark. In any case, we can
make use of this Trojan, for we shall soon be able to
make him talk. Let him pass, then we can cut off his
retreat."

So the two Greeks hid behind a broken chariot, and the
Trojan walked by without suspecting their presence, for
his mind was occupied with thoughts of the splendid
rewards that would be given him if he succeeded in his
mission.

Suddenly he leapt forward and began to run at great
speed for two men had rushed towards him, and he
realised that they were enemies.

Then Diomedes threw his javelin and it grazed the
shoulder of the fugitive. "Stop," cried the Greek. "That
was only a warning. The next one will pin you to the
ground."

Half-dead with fear and trembling in every limb, the

Trojan turned round and crouched down at the feet of his pursuers. "Spare me," he said in beseeching tones. "If you will spare me, I will give you a rich ransom."

"Have no fear," replied Ulysses. "If you will speak freely you can save your life. Tell us where is Hector and what are his plans? How are the sentries posted? Tell us all you know or I will ram my sword down your throat."

More dead than alive, the unfortunate captive reported that Hector was in council with his chieftains near the tomb of Ilus; his allies were sleeping whilst the Trojan soldiers kept watch.

"But," added the man, "if you would find some rich booty without too many difficulties, make your way to the west side of our camp, towards the quarters of the Thracians, who are under the command of King Rhesus. He has a splendid chariot plated with gold and silver and swift horses, whiter than snow."

"Be silent," interrupted Diomedes impatiently. "We have heard all that we desire to know, but you talk much too freely for us to spare your life. How can we respect a man who betrays his country. Now die, you cowardly traitor."

And, without letting himself be moved by a plea for mercy made by Ulysses, Diomedes thrust his sword through the body of the Trojan.

"We must advance with all speed towards the Thracian quarters," murmured Ulysses, "so that we can bring back some proof that we have carried out our mission."

Swiftly and silently, they crept towards the tents occupied by Rhesus and his followers. The King and his men were so heavy with sleep that they did not hear the Greeks moving towards them. Nearby, the horses, unharnessed, were grazing in the centre of the encampment, guarded on all sides by lines of sleeping men whose weapons were arranged on the ground.

"Ulysses," whispered Diomedes, "those white horses with their heads turned towards us certainly belong to Rhesus. Cut their hobbles whilst I deal with the soldiers. Go now, and may Minerva help us both!"

Ulysses crept so quietly in between the slumbering Thracians that not one of them awoke. In a trice he had unhobbled the horses and led them out towards Diomedes. The latter then stooped over the recumbant warriors, who quickly passed from the sleep of life to the sleep of death.

At last some of them were roused by the groans and cries of their neighbours, and they attempted to take up their arms, but Diomedes did not give them time to do so, and he succeeded in despatching more of their number.

Then, still athirst for blood, he rushed into the tent of Rhesus and killed him, whilst Ulysses mounted one of the white horses. In the meantime, every man in the camp had heard the unfortunate King's cry of agony and was prepared to take action. "Comrade," cried Ulysses, "come to your senses. You have already avenged yesterday's defeat. We must fly before it is too late!" At last Diomedes relented and, leaping upon the horse which Ulysses held in readiness for him, they both set off at a full gallop. A shower of arrows made the sand spurt up behind them, but neither of the fugitives was struck. They came near to the Greek camp as the first rays of the morning revealed to them the warriors and chieftains standing by the main gate and anxiously awaiting their return.

As soon as they were recognised, a great shout of welcome arose to greet them.

"Wise Ulysses, and you brave Diomedes," cried Nestor. "I see that you have succeeded in penetrating into the enemy's lines. Assuredly, Greece can never be vanquished whilst she has such men as you to defend her. You have behaved like gods rather than men."

"Venerable Nestor," replied Ulysses, staggering with fatigue, "your praise fills us with pride, but indeed we are sorry-looking gods. See, Diomedes is dripping with sweat and I am as hungry as any mortal can be."

Everyone hastened to attend to their needs. The two warriors bathed and then were rubbed down with oil to take the stiffness out of their limbs; after which they sat down to a banquet provided by Nestor.

Scarcely had they finished eating when there was a loud peal of trumpets and immediately the chieftains fell to arms. Agamemnon, wearing his shining breastplate and climbing into his chariot, placed himself at the head of his army.

First came the chariots of the chieftains spread out in a line behind the protecting trench. Behind them were ranged all the foot-soldiers, with the horsemen in array on either side. Opposite the Greeks, the Trojans also formed into battle order, whilst Hector, his armour flashing in the rays of the sun, inspected his men.

Then, like reapers advancing across a field of ripe wheat to mow it down, the two armies charged against each other. The first clash of arms turned in favour of the Trojans, but the Greeks soon rallied, and the exploits of their great commander, Agamemnon, made them shout with joy. The Trojans then began to run away in great disorder, and even Hector could not induce them to face up to their enemies, but he remained confident, for a voice whispered in his ear: "To-day, before night has cast its long dark shadows over the earth, I will grant you victory."

He determined therefore to prevent the defeat of the Trojans from turning into a complete rout, and did everything in his power to harass Agamemnon, so that he might avenge the death of several of his brothers, who had been killed by the Greek Commander. Suddenly he uttered a cry of joy, for a javelin had just pierced Agamemnon's right arm, and he staggered back in his chariot and dropped his lance.

"Eurymedion," he said falteringly to his driver. "Urge on the horses and take me back to my tent. I am in great pain and I can no longer stand." Speedily Eurymedion wheeled his chariot around and crossed the plain at a full gallop. When they reached the camp he helped his master into his tent. All those who had seen him pass by were filled with anxiety, for they knew the soldiers would miss the leadership of their commander.

Indeed, the Trojans had already taken courage. "Agamemnon is wounded!" cried Hector. "Men, victory is ours. Follow me and we shall surely win."

On hearing Hector's words, the Trojans rallied,

charged and began to regain the ground that they had lost. The Greeks now fell one after another, by tens, by scores and by hundreds. If Ulysses and Diomedes had not barred the way, the Trojans would assuredly have reached the Greek ships and set them on fire. In spite of Hector's superhuman courage, the valour of his two adversaries halted his headlong advance.

Alas, the gods favoured the Trojans on that fateful day! Leaning on the tomb of Ilus, the great ancestor of his race, Paris was watching Diomedes, bow in hand. Twice he let fly one of his shafts, but without success. Then came the fateful moment. An arrow whistled through the air, pierced the right foot of Diomedes and pinned it to the ground. "Ulysses," cried the hero in great agony. "Protect me with your shield, so that I may pull this arrow out of my foot and continue the fight."

Paris rushed towards Diomedes sword in hand, crying "Since you are wounded, victory is ours."

Clenching his teeth with a cry of pain, Diomedes succeeded in pulling out the arrow which was tearing his flesh, and whilst Ulysses helped him back into his chariot, he retorted scornfully to Paris: "You have done me no real injury; the shafts of cowards do little harm. Soon you will feel mine, for when we meet face to face the lightest wound from my javelin will bring about your death. No longer admired by women, your body will be the carion of vultures and ravens."

His angry words were drowned by the noise of his chariot as he set off at full gallop. Around him the Greeks were taking flight, and before long the courageous Ulysses remained alone on the plain, battling against a large number of adversaries.

"O gods of Olympus," he sighed, striking out on all sides and felling to the ground those who came too near him, "is this my end? I cannot run away, for that would be shameful, and yet I seem to be facing up alone to the whole of Troy. What will become of me?"

The Trojans surrounded him. There was a clash of steel on breastplates and shields; then blood began to flow, for a lance thrust had wounded Ulysses in the flank. A mist began to cloud his eyes, but he would not give way, determined that no Trojan should have his arms as trophy. Three times he uttered a rending cry for help and he pierced an enemy with his lance as he was attacking him with upraised sword.

Menelaus and Ajax recognised the voice of their friend and rushed forward to drag him away from the Trojans, who were surrounding him like a pack of hounds. But soon they had to give way in their turn and prudently retreat to their own camp, taking the wounded man with them. As for Hector, everyone gave way before him; even Ajax himself dared not come face to face with him.

Slowly, covering the retreat of the Greeks, the hero battled on only giving way when he was overwhelmed by the constant attacks of his enemies. The ditch and the wall, those frail protections of the Greek camp, were not calculated to stop the advance of the aggressors for long, nor to give confidence to the defeated. Even the corner towers began to creak, shaking beneath the blows of the Trojans.

"It is our fault," cried the haggard and despairing soldiers of Agamemnon. "Did we not put up these walls without consulting the gods, without offering up sacrifices to them. They hate these fortifications and they have sworn to destroy them. It is no use persisting in defending them. Let us retreat to our ships instead."

The greatest confusion and disorder prevailed throughout the camp. Nearly all the Greek leaders were wounded and incapable of controlling the panic and terror which had overcome their men, since they believed they had offended the gods, who had therefore decreed their downfall.

Despite the confusion among the enemy, Hector and his allies did not dare to attempt an assault on the ditch and the wall without carefully considering how it should best be done. Swiftly they consulted together, for they thought perhaps that this rapid flight of the Greeks was intended to draw them into an ambush.

"Let us abandon our chariots," said Hector, "for the space between the ditch and the wall is too narrow to allow them to manœuvre, and then it would be easy for the Greeks to drive us back into the trench. We must leave our horses here. We shall be less encumbered if we rely on our weapons and our shields to protect us. Take courage, comrades, and follow me, for Jupiter is on our side and will grant us victory."

Divided into three columns, the Trojans began their assault with their shields closely set together to form a wall of bronze. Inspired with high hopes, they felt that the enemy was already beaten and his fleet destroyed.

From the top of their towers, the Greeks showered

down arrows and stones on the attackers. The earth seemed afire, and long echoes of arrows and javelins clashing against shields and helmets resounded through the plain.

From above, in the peace of Olympus, the gods looked down upon great human tragedy with quivering hearts.

5

The Death of Patrocles

RESSING forward with all the fury of a great tempest, the Trojans rushed towards the walls. The first of their men fell beneath the missiles of the defenders, but Hector's voice continued to encourage his men.

"Forward," he cried. "Scale the ramparts. Victory is already ours." And he himself rushed towards the doorway in the wall through which the Greek army had just passed in headlong flight. An iron bar kept the door in place, but Hector made light of such an obstacle. Stooping down, he seized a huge block of rock and threw it right into the woodwork, which was immediately shattered. There was a cry of despair among the Greeks, whilst, following Hector closely, the assailants rushed through the splintered door. Agamemnon's men were overcome with terror. Scarcely defending themselves, and in spite of the shouts and commands of Ajax, who was one of the few surviving leaders, they streamed in headlong flight towards their ships.

Ajax gathered round him the few men who had not been seized by panic: "Let us die courageously," he cried. "Let us sell our lives dearly." The heroic phalanx advanced in wedge formation against their enemies, who faced them with over-confidence. So little did they expect resistance that, on seeing the column bristling with spears, they checked their advance, and Ajax immediately took advantage of this setback by collecting and rallying a number of fugitives whom he had shamed out of their panic. Then, for a while, all the efforts of Hector, Paris, Aeneas and other Trojan commanders failed before the indomitable courage of the Greeks.

"Come, chieftains," cried Ajax in a loud voice. "Forget your wounds and your fatigue or our ships will be destroyed." Menelaus and other Greek commanders, with blood still streaming from their wounds, obeyed this brave summons and mustered their soldiers, for they realised that, whatever the cost, they must prevent Hector from advancing towards their right wing, for it was in that direction that the ships of Ajax and his commanders were beached. If they were set on fire, the flames would leap from one vessel to another and the whole fleet would be consumed.

So the battle continued with increased fury. The tumult was tremendous. Amid the cries of the dying the voices of Hector and Ajax rose, encouraging their men and challenging their opponents.

"Come, come, Hector," scoffed Ajax. "You cannot

make the Greeks tremble with empty threats. The time is coming when you will flee in your turn."

"You madman!" replied Hector with a taunting laugh. "It is you who will have to retreat still further, and then I will throw your body into the sea."

Overcome with weariness and exhausted by their wounds, Agamemnon, Diomedes and Ulysses sadly watched the different phases of the battle. "O gods," cried Agamemnon, rousing himself painfully, "the Trojans have broken through our walls. What can our soldiers be doing? The enemy is occupying our camp."

The despair that was overwhelming them increased further when they were joined by Nestor, who came up with bowed head. "We must fly," said Agamemnon. "That is all that we can do now. We must drag our ships into the sea, and as night is beginning to fall, the darkness will hide our departure from the Trojans. Certainly some of us will not escape, and our flight in the darkness is not without danger, but to ensure that even a small part of our nation avoids destruction we must take this risk."

Ulysses looked disdainfully at his commander. Then, wiping away the sweat which flowed from his brow with a strip of his cloak, he expressed his indignation: "How dare you give us such shameful advice?" said he. "Take care that the other Greeks do not hear you or they will blush with shame on your behalf. If we run away, we complete the triumph of the Trojans. Let us go forward and fight to our last breath."

"Yes," cried Diomedes impetuously. "However wounded and tired we may be, however helpless to wield our swords, we can surely give our men renewed courage by our presence."

His advice was followed without delay. Hastening as best they could and supporting themselves on their spears, the three leaders limped towards the fray.

The mere sight of them did indeed help to restore the courage of the Greeks. Many of the fugitives returned, and after having exchanged their broken or blunted weapons for those of the fallen, they gathered round to form a living barrier between their opponents and their ships.

"Comrades," cried Nestor in a beseeching voice, "spare us the shame of seeing the decks of our ships, the benches of our oarsmen sullied by the feet of our enemies." Three times in succession Hector launched his soldiers against the wall of bronze formed by the shields of the remaining Greeks. The slaughter was greater than ever, and men on either side were roused to fight with equal fury. Even Ulysses no longer felt the weariness that had overcome him and, with great care, he fitted an arrow to his bow and took skilful aim at Hector's muscular frame, but the latter seemed to be under the protection of the King of all the gods, for not a single arrow even struck the shining breastplate of the Trojan hero. All around the princes, his brothers, and other officers fell beneath the shafts aimed unerringly by Ulysses and Ajax, but the great champion of Troy, scorning death that threatened him all the time, continued to charge on the Greek phalanxes with more determination than ever.

"Since this human wall cannot be opened like the

gates of the rampart," he shouted after his third on-slaught, "we will leap over it. Have not the gods promised that we shall set fire to every ship this very day! The gods cannot lie. Follow me!!" And with a lithe and immense bound the champion leapt over the first rank of the Greeks.

Loud shouts of applause and rage greeted this mag-nificent action. Overcome by this unforeseen manœuvre, Ajax was so bewildered that Hector could deal his death blows to right and left without encountering any firm resistance. This time there was real panic. Carried away by the rout of their men and sobbing with despair, the Greek chieftains were thrown back against the ships of Ajax and his followers.

Bellowing with anger, Ajax climbed upon a bench and challenged to combat. So great was the tumult that the trembling supplication of Nestor could not even be heard, and in vain the old man besought the Greeks to remember that they were fighting for the safety of their nation and for the honour of their name.

Now Hector had rushed upon a vessel, torch in hand, for he wished to be the first to set fire to the ships of his hated foe, but Ajax tore the flaming brand from his grasp and threw it into the sand, turning round with the nimble-ness of a panther to strike down a Trojan who was about to set his ship alight.

"Comrades," shouted out Ajax. "Fight to the death, for our fate is at stake. No one can help us if we do not save ourselves."

Words cannot fully describe the fearful spectacle of the battle fought so desperately around the ships, for not a

Greek could have watched unmoved the imminent ruin of all their dearest hopes. If the fleet had really been set alight, the men of the defeated army would never be able to see again the scented shores of their own beautiful land. Not a man would escape death, or if he did so, no place of refuge would be open to him.

At the far end of the camp, with ears straining to hear how the tide of battle turned, Patrocles, faithful friend of Achilles, had raised the flap of his tent whilst his King and comrade continued to play heedlessly on his lyre.

Patrocles could no longer watch unmoved the outcome of this mighty struggle in which his greatest enemies were about to be triumphant. Was he not a Greek? And all the greatest and noblest warriors of Greece were about to die on this barbarian shore. Wringing his hands, he turned towards his friend and cried out in a broken voice: "O, Achilles, are you indeed determined that our brothers shall perish without making the slightest movement to help them? The most valiant of our Greek chieftains are dying or wounded, the enemy is in our camp. Can you not see the mighty Hector brandishing a flaming torch. O gods of Olympus, the rigging of a ship is already alight. Can your anger be so great that it prevents you from rushing into battle?

"I know indeed that the oracle foretold that you would die in front of the walls of Troy, but if that holds you back give me your armour so that they may take me for you and I may lead them into battle. This alone will save the Greeks. Give me, I implore you, the opportunity to preserve them from complete destruction."

Now, although Achilles was still dominated by his

resentment, he could not remain completely unmoved by the peril that threatened his fatherland. With a sharp gesture, he beckoned to his squires to bring his armour and give it to Patrocles, together with his huge shield and sharp sword. He placed his shining helmet with its long plume of horsehair on the head of his friend. Then he embraced him. "Patrocles," he said gently, "go, since you wish it, and I wish it too, but return to me soon. Do not venture beyond the confines of the camp, for you need do no more than drive the Trojans out of it. Do not let your ardour bear you as far as the walls of Troy, for I am filled with a sad foreboding at the thought of it. Leave for me the glory of storming and capturing the city at such time as I decide to forgive Agamemnon. Dear Patrocles, take every care, for I shall need you with me when I launch my attack against the impregnable walls of Ilium."

After listening to those words, Patrocles sped swiftly from the tent and summoned the soldiers of his chief. "Men, follow me. You have murmured long enough at being idle. Now you will have the opportunity to show the fullness of your courage."

A long and loud cheer greeted this call to arms, for the Myrmidons were only too eager to prove their worth. Immediately Patrocles leapt into the chariot of Achilles, which Automedon, the King's own driver, had brought to rest in front of him.

The splendid white horses were celebrated because of their speed and their endurance. Indeed, their beauty was such that men said that they must have been bred in the land of the gods, for were they not faster and stronger

" It is not you, Hector, who kill me, it is the gods"

than any other steeds? Achilles, who was witnessing the scene from afar, poured out a cup of wine as a libation and besought Jupiter to grant victory to his men and bring them back safely to their quarters.

As it befell, the King of the gods was to grant only half of this request. Nevertheless, on seeing Patrocles, whom they took for Achilles, the Trojans were seized with fear, whilst the Greeks uttered cries of joy and began to fight with renewed vigour.

The newcomers threw themselves joyously into the fray, and soon their enemies began to give way and scatter. The first javelin thrown by Patrocles killed Pyrechmes, King of the Peonias and one of the most valiant allies of Troy. His death dismayed his followers, and their headlong flight forced the Trojans to withdraw swiftly, so as not to be surrounded. "Victory is ours," cried Diomedes. Jumping into his chariot, he galloped off after Patrocles, who was hotly pursuing his foes.

By now the fire that had begun to spread through the ships had been controlled and extinguished. The Greeks then breathed more freely and their courage returned.

Although they were scattered and giving way rapidly, the Trojans still continued to resist fiercely: javelins flew through the air, valiant men died from lance-thrusts or were cut down mercilessly by their foes. Ajax had set off in pursuit of Hector, whilst Patrocles, heedless of the warning of Achilles, advanced in the same direction.

"Stop," he cried on catching sight of the Trojan hero, whose horses were flecked with foam. "Stop. For I must take vengeance for all the Greeks whom you have killed."

6

As Hector was not able to rein in his horses that Patrocles might overtake him, the Greek now vented his wrath on all the Trojans within reach. One after another their champions fell before his relentless sword, until finally he was faced by Sarpedon, the most valiant of the Trojan chiefs save Hector.

He tried to attack Patrocles, but his lance slipped in his hands, so he only succeeded in wounding one of the chariot horses of Achilles. Automedon made his team rear up on their hind legs, whilst Patrocles stooped and threw his javelin, striking his adversary full in the chest.

"Your arms are my trophies, Sarpedon," cried Patrocles, jumping down from his horse to strip the conquered chieftain of his weapons.

But whilst he was bending over the recumbant body, a loud cry from his followers made him look up. Hector had heard of the death of his friend, and he had become maddened with grief and resentment. Come what may, he would save the hallowed remains of the Trojan hero and, mastering his horses with a great effort, he forced them back into the fray.

"Fight on, men," he cried to the Trojans. "The Greeks can still be defeated!"

The battle continued to rage more fiercely than ever round the battered body of Sarpedon, in order to protect his weapons and his armour—spoils without which no champion could ever be considered to be truly victorious. On perceiving Hector close by, Patrocles refused to fight any longer for mere trophies. The safety of Greece was more dear to him by far than his pride as a soldier. He therefore drove his chariot towards Hector.

Perhaps it was from caution or for tactical reasons, but the latter wheeled his chariot round and galloped off towards Troy at full speed. On seeing his adversary retreating, Patrocles cast aside all prudence.

"Come," he said to Automedon, who advised him to be cautious, reminding him of the warnings of Achilles. "Drive on! The great Hector is in my power!"

Thus, filled with pride and determination, Patrocles leant forward as though he would outstrip the swift gallop of his horses.

Suddenly Hector wheeled round and drove straight towards Patrocles. The latter threw his javelin, but Hector turned his head aside, and it was his driver, Cerion, who received the mortal blow and rolled down into the dust.

"Ah," cried Patrocles. "I thought that I was fighting against men and not against puppets."

Then he jumped to the ground, and Hector followed his example, so that they were soon engaged in a deadly hand-to-hand combat. Around them the battle still continued; arrows and javelins whistled through the air; there was the clashing of weapon against weapon, and weapon against the bronze shields of the warriors. Neither of the champions gave way or showed any sign of yielding. Indeed, the soldiers on each side rushed into the fray with the same fierce courage.

The sun was already high in the heavens, but the tide of battle still remained undecided. In Olympus, on the mountaintop, the scales held by Jupiter, King of the gods, were evenly balanced in the hands of the master of all destinies.

Nine warriors had already been struck down by Patrocles when suddenly, as if Apollo, patron of Hector, had intervened, the friend and henchman of Achilles staggered. His plumed helmet rolled in the dust beneath his horses' feet; his pike broke in his hands; the heavy shield broke free from his wrist and fell; the straps of his breastplate were loosened as if by an invisible hand.

Patrocles wiped the sweat from his streaming brow with trembling fingers and was seized with a dreadful foreboding. He tried to run away, but all movement had become impossible, so he remained with his feet rooted to the ground, helpless and motionless.

A Trojan passed behind the hero and pierced his shoulder with a stroke of his sword. In spite of the grave pain, Patrocles did not fall, and he raised his unarmed hand threateningly towards Hector, who was approaching with upraised sword.

"It is not you, Hector, who kill me," he said proudly. "It is the gods. Ah, had it been only the Trojans fighting against me it would have been an easy matter, but I have been vanquished by the Immortals who govern our destinies."

The sword of his adversary sank into his breast up to the hilt and he fell to the ground. His eyes closed slowly, and little by little his soul deserted him to set forth on the long journey to the Kingdom of the Shadows.

"Vengeance will be swift," he murmured. "My death will be upon your head and destiny is already sharpening the sword of Achilles." So saying, he died, and Hector stood as though overwhelmed by the weight of his victory.

So astonished was he that Automedon galloped off un-
noticed and thus saved his master's chariot from falling
into enemy hands, whilst at the same time he saved his
own life.

Menelaus saw the well-known team of horses pass by
like a flash. "Where is Patrocles?" he cried to Automedon, but the latter's face, bathed in tears, was sufficient indication of what had happened. Then did Menelaus, only possessed by a desire for vengeance, rush to the
place where the hero had fallen. He saw before him
Euphorbus, the Trojan who had first wounded Patrocles
and so coveted his arms as trophies. The Greek raised his
arm and struck his adversary in the throat with his sword,
so that his body fell streaming with blood on the corpse
of the friend so beloved of Achilles. But Hector now faced
Menelaus and, surrounded by a score of Trojans, the
Greek King was forced to give way.

Suddenly he heard an exclamation of joy. Ajax was
there close at hand fighting fiercely at the head of his
men. "Ajax! Ajax!" he cried. "Help! Patrocles is dead.
We must save his body from desecration."

Swiftly Ajax came to his side, and together the two
chieftains launched themselves upon Hector who, sword
in hand, was about to cut off the head of the dead Greek.
On seeing the Greek champions, he hesitated and then
stepped back.

"Come," he shouted to his followers. "Carry into the
city the armour which I have won in fair combat. I will
put it on and thus shame and deride the Greeks."

Stepping up into his chariot, he reached the gates of
the city in a few minutes. Whilst putting on the breast-

plate of Achilles and tying the shield of the hero to his wrist he perceived that Menelaus and Ajax had at last gained possession of the body of Patrocles, and that they were trying to carry it away from the battlefield. Hector frowned. If the remains of the Greek escaped, would he not lose much of the fame of his victory? He uttered a loud cry.

"Trojans!" he shouted to those who had accompanied him. "Return to the fray. We must complete the defeat of the Greeks. The man who recaptures the body of Patrocles and brings it back into the city can have his share of my glory!"

So once more this band of Trojans rushed out to battle against the Greeks, and so great was their number that both Menelaus and Ajax thought that their last day had come. Yet did they not give way. They laid their dead friend's body, for which they were risking their lives, upon the ground and carefully protected it with their shields whilst their comrades stood around them, swearing that rather would they die than surrender the glorious remains of the hero who had turned the tide of battle.

Hours passed: the fighting was more bitter than ever. The Greeks were now fighting, not for their lives, but for their honour. What greater inspiration did they need?

Victory favoured first one side, then the other. Sometimes the Greeks were forced to retreat and abandon the body that they were defending; at others they were able to recapture it and drive back the Trojans. The walls of Troy, over which they had fought for ten years, the ships of the Greeks, which had so nearly been destroyed, were all forgotten in the face of this one ambition—to gain possession of the remains of Patrocles. It seemed that Jupiter was taking pleasure in granting success in turn to each of the battling armies. By his order, the Furies and Discord raged among the combatants, firing their ardour, urging them on against each other and encouraging them to continue the dreadful slaughter.

Minerva and Apollo joined in the fray. Their mysterious and powerful voices revived the warriors and aroused the enthusiasms of Greeks and Trojans. "It is our duty to tell Achilles the grievous news," said Menelaus to Ajax in the midst of the fighting. "If he knew what had happened, might he not come to our aid now and help us to victory?"

"We must rely on our own efforts," said Ajax harshly. "Achilles has lost his armour and cannot fight. But see, Menelaus, the Trojans are giving way. Carry away the body of Patrocles with the help of Meriones. We will guard your retreat and protect you with our shields!"

Obeying this advice, the two warriors took the body in their arms whilst Ajax redoubled his efforts in their defence. Around him the Greeks had formed an impenetrable barrier and, in spite of the valiant efforts of Hector, in spite of the taunting shouts of the Trojans who were enraged to see their prey escape, the remains of Patrocles were soon placed on the chariot of Menelaus. Panting with fatigue, but happy and proud to have succeeded in the appointed task, Menelaus and Meriones stood in the chariot urging on their horses, who set off at a gallop.

Behind them, Ajax and his men were forced by their weariness to retreat rapidly so as to shelter behind the trench which encircled their camp. The Trojans pursued them closely, shouting out: "We know how to reach your ships. This time Patrocles will not be there to save you from defeat."

6

The Sorrows of Achilles

CHILLES had remained seated at the threshold of his tent, straining his ears for the dread sounds of battle. He had seen that Patrocles had not contented himself with driving the enemy out of the camp, and he was filled with anxiety for his friend fighting beneath the walls of Ilium and surrounded by perils.

"How could I allow him to go?" he said to himself sadly. "Why did I not accompany him? Wretch that I am, I allowed myself to be possessed by obstinate resentment rather than listen to the calls of friendship. O Jupiter, if there is yet time, deign to protect Patrocles from the dread horror of death."

For hours Achilles continued to pray, but all in vain, for his friend was already one of the stark dead bodies that lay scattered on the plain.

Suddenly Antilochus appeared, out of breath and with his face showing the greatest sorrow. Achilles cried out, and then gave him a questioning look.

"Yes," said the messenger with bowed head, "Patrocles is indeed dead and your arms are in Hector's hands. The mangled remains of your friend are in danger of being carried off by the Trojans."

Achilles fell back, uttering rending cries. He rolled in the dust, tearing his hair and his clothes, and in vain did Antilochus console him. Around them slaves and servants sorrowfully watched the despair of their master and besought him not to take his own life, but Achilles would not listen, for he was given up entirely to his grief.

In the depths of the sea, in the palace of rock and seaweed where she dwelt among the nymphs and the syrens, Thetis, his mother, goddess of the sea, had heard of the great bereavement which had befallen her son. Making herself invisible, she flew to him and took him in her arms.

"O my son," she said to him, "what can I do to relieve the depth of your misery? Calm your despair, I implore you. Alas, destiny is stronger than we are. Flee from this accursed shore or you will perish too."

"No," said Achilles hoarsely. "I wish to avenge my friend, my companion whom I have lost. What can death matter to me? For now life is distasteful to me. O my mother, why did you encourage me in my resentment? Had it not kept me inactive, I should have remained at the head of the Greeks. I should have repelled the onslaught of the Trojans, and Patrocles, my dear Patrocles, would still be alive. I must kill Hector, the murderer of my friend and, even should I die, I shall regret nothing."

Thetis kissed her son on the brow and sighed deeply but she did not trÿ to weaken his determination. "Wait for me," she said. "You will need weapons if you are going to fight, and the gods alone can forge them. The sun is about to sink into the sea and the darkness of the night will cause the fighting to cease. Already the clash of arms is dying down. To-morrow at early dawn I will bring you arms worthy of your valour."

Shortly afterwards, Menelaus and Meriones drove up, bringing the body of Patrocles. Achilles rushed out and, on seeing the remains of his friend, gave full vent to his feelings. "I will avenge you, Patrocles," he swore solemnly, "and I will join you in the Kingdom of Darkness. The blood of Hector will not be sufficient to complete my vengeance, and so I will sacrifice with my own hands twelve young Trojans on your funeral pyre."

Whilst Achilles was filling the air with his lamentations, the Thessalonian warriors washed the body of Patrocles and covered it with a shroud. All night long they gathered around their prince and mourned with his beloved friend.

Scarcely had dawn opened the pearly gates of the eastern skies when Thetis, faithful to her promise, appeared before Achilles.

"O my son," she said tenderly, "this is not the time to give way to vain tears. See these arms that I have brought you. The divine Vulcan himself has forged them. Five broad strips of copper and of gold form the shield, and on this buckler the god has chiselled all the marvels of the world; the earth with all its men and many other things besides. The gods themselves appear on it in all their glory; the woods, the plains, the mountains are displayed upon it in all their delight. Let me place upon your head this dazzling helmet with its plume of gold, and press upon your body this breastplate, more brilliant than fire itself. Take this sword! Vulcan has forged it in twenty furnaces, taming the winds to serve him instead of bellows. See how it shines! My son, which of your enemies will be bold enough to fix their eyes on the blinding glitter of your arms. Are you not proud to be the only man to own these masterpieces made by a god? Console yourself now and weep no more."

Achilles looked with admiration and pride at these resplendent weapons and his soldier's heart was filled with sad joy. "My thanks to you, O mother, for with these gifts from the gods I can see to it that the ghost of Patrocles will be able to wander at peace through the Elysian Fields."

Then, with eyes burning with a fierce light, he summoned his soldiers and advanced towards the ships of his allies, who were assembled in a council of war. On seeing Achilles coming towards them, they stood up and greeted him with shouts of welcome.

"Glory to Achilles," said Ulysses, advancing towards him with outstretched hands. "Blessed be the gods who in our days of sorrow know how to bring us a harvest of joy."

Achilles nodded and said in a sad but firm voice: "Agamemnon, let us forget if possible our mistakes and our losses. Had there not been this fatal discord between us, many of our valiant soldiers would still be alive, but we must not put our pride before the needs of our country.

Order our men to go into battle and I will go with them. I will pursue the Trojans to the very walls of Troy, and this time I swear that Hector will not escape."

The Greeks applauded these words with great delight, and then Agamemnon rose to his feet and called for silence. "Achilles," he said without the usual note of pride, "I thank you. Your return fills all the Greeks with joy and makes us forget our past misfortunes."

"Nevertheless, I feel that we are not responsible for the quarrel that broke out between us. It was the gods and the hand of Destiny that made us lose all reason and brought error into our hearts. In me they aroused the fatal desire to do you an injury, and in you your lasting resentment. I wish to repair as much as possible the harm that I have done. All the presents about which I spoke to Ulysses shall be brought to you forthwith. Briseis shall return to you, and I have done her no harm. Indeed, she was treated with all the consideration due to the promised bride of the great Achilles."

At a sign from Agamemnon, the gifts were placed before him. The gold of the tripods and of the jars shone with great brilliance. Twelve splendid Thracian horses were held back with difficulty by their grooms, and seven young slave girls bowed their lovely heads respectfully before the mightiest champion of the Greeks. Near them stood Briseis smiling timidly.

"Briseis," murmured Achilles. "So you are here, my well-beloved. Alas, that the joy of seeing you cannot make me forget my sorrow." Achilles sighed; then, frowning sternly, he continued in a voice heavy with anger: "I will avenge my friend without delay. Even before the flames have finished consuming his ashes on the funeral pyre, Hector shall die. And you, Agamemnon, together with all the heroes of Greece, I summon you to battle. Even though you are weakened from hunger, worn out by your great efforts, you must fight on. We shall only cease from battle when the enemy has been completely vanquished. You must call forth all your might and courage if you wish to follow me in this great venture."

Agamemnon applauded this brave appeal to the Greeks. "To arms!" he cried. "Order your chariots to be harnessed. We must follow Achilles with all speed!"

But Ulysses came up to the two kings, and took them by the hand. "Achilles," he said, "you are bolder and stronger than I, but I have the advantage of age and of experience, and so I have the right to advise you, since you are younger. Fasting soldiers soon become exhausted and lose their aggressiveness. If we wish to avenge our dead we must be strong and hearty. Come, let us sit down to a banquet. Then shall we fight all the better, and not one of us will lag behind. Wine makes our limbs more lithe and brings courage to our hearts."

Hastily tables were set out in the camp, whilst the slaves prepared rich food and poured the wine into goblets of silver and of gold, so that the Greek chieftains could offer up libations to the gods. Agamemnon and Achilles swore eternal friendship and a white bull was sacrificed to seal their reconciliation.

Soon the Greeks were seated, restoring their strength with food and wine so as to be ready and alert for the coming struggle. Achilles alone had not followed their example. Seated near them, but overwhelmed by his immense grief, he waited impatiently for the end of this banquet.

At last Agamemnon rose and gave the signal for departure, mustering all the warriors at his command. Who would have thought seeing them now, firm and resolute, only the day before they had been ready to accept defeat!

Clad in his splendid armour, with his brilliantly plumed helmet on his head, bearing in one hand his wondrous shield and in the other the spear that no warrior but he could wield, Achilles drove in his chariot at the head of the Greek army.

Suddenly, uttering a wild cry, which echoed all around him, he urged on his white horses, and the men behind him followed eagerly. There before them, lined up on the plain, the Trojans were awaiting attack.

Fierce fighting broke out and no mercy was shown by either side. However, Hector avoided Achilles, who was searching for him. Perhaps his protector, Apollo, had whispered to him that he should not fight against his Greek rival at this hour and, frightened by this warning, the Trojan had taken refuge among his men.

In the meantime, Achilles displayed great courage and astonishing skill in attacking his enemies. Spurning the foot-soldiers, he turned on their chiefs, striking them down from their chariots with his spear and laughing fiercely he struck out to the right and to the left, with each blow killing a foe.

Before him the Trojans ran in headlong flight. Seized with panic, they deserted this plain where only the day before Hector had triumphantly spread terror and destruction.

Continuing to attack with great fury, Achilles drove some of the Trojans towards the banks of the swiftly-flowing Xanthe, and forced many of them into the water, where they were drowned.

The bulk of their army did not halt until the soldiers could take shelter behind the ramparts of their city, but they left behind many of their number dead or wounded on the plain. However, Hector, who had achieved miracles in protecting the retreat of his countrymen, now paused outside the principal gate of Troy.

Priam, who had been watching the progress of the fighting from the battlements of the ramparts, came down and clutched his son desperately by the arm. "Beloved Hector," he moaned, "why stay outside this gate? Come into the city and rest for a while in your palace, but do not match your strength against the invincible Achilles. Preserve your life for other things, for, however great our losses have been, I do not mourn whilst you remain to uphold and guide our nation." Priam wept and bent his white head over the hand of his son, and Queen Hecuba came to join her husband in trying to persuade Hector from going out to fight Achilles.

"Take pity on your mother," she said. "Do not challenge this fierce enemy. If he killed you, Andromache would not be able to give your body an honourable funeral. Dear Hector, think of your countrymen and their dreadful plight. What would become of them if you were to die? All the men would be slaughtered, and the women and children would be carried off into slavery. For their sake, have pity on us!"

Although his heart was torn at the sight of his mother's

Achilles had ordered his men to tie the feet of Hector to his chariot

great distress, although his eyes strayed over the rooftops which sheltered his wife and his son, Hector did not give way. How could he display such cowardice? "Better by far," he thought, "to fight and die like a hero."

Hector had scarcely made up his mind than Achilles appeared before him, fierce and threatening, gripping his mighty spear in his fist. The Trojan bounded into his chariot and drove off at full speed towards the mouth of the River Xanthe, but Achilles began to catch up with him.

From their dwelling above, the gods watched this strange pursuit with great emotion, for no one could tell how it would end. As for Jupiter, he was distressed that he could not save Hector from his sad fate, but he dared not stay the remorseless decrees of Destiny, whilst Minerva, still invisible, followed the two rivals in their mad race in order to stir up their hatred for each other.

Finally, the Greek champion caught up his adversary, and the latter, realising that he was in great danger, turned to face his foe.

"O Achilles," he cried, leaping to the ground. "You saw me fleeing before you, but I will flee no more. I shall kill you or be killed by you. Nevertheless, let us make a pact: let not our hatred continue beyond the grave. If I am the victor, I will content myself with claiming your armour and your weapons, but I will give back your body to the Greeks. This, I swear, and now I ask you to do the same."

"Never," said Achilles, grinding his teeth with rage. "You killed Patrocles! No oath could possibly bind me to you. Your death or mine—that is all that I ask for. You will need all your courage, for Minerva is about to kill you by my hand."

With irresistible force, he threw himself towards Hector, and his javelin flew through the air, grazing the head of the Trojan. The latter lunged with his sword and struck the shield of Achilles so terrible a blow that his weapon fell from his hand.

Hector turned pale: for now he was unarmed, as he had dropped his spear in the flight, but there still remained his javelin, which he prepared to throw. Before he could do so, the sword of Achilles penetrated a joint in his armour and pierced him through and through. Hector fell to the ground mortally wounded.

He lay there stretched out on the sand and, though his eyes were beginning to cloud, he gazed through a mist at the land for which he had fought so bravely, watching the white clouds glide across the blue sky and listening to the rushing waters of the river.

"O my fatherland, O my loved ones, must I leave you so soon?" he murmured.

Achilles bent over him and said scornfully: "Now, bold conqueror! When you slew Patrocles, you did not stop to consider that I was still alive. The Greeks will pay due honour to the ashes of your victim, whilst your body will remain here to be the carrion of dogs and vultures."

"For the sake of mercy," faltered Hector, "grant my loved ones at least the sad joy of burying me with ceremony. Give back my body to Priam and to Andromache."

"No," roared Achilles! "There can be no pity for you. Die, die in despair!"

"Relentless man," sighed Hector. "Take heed of the vengeance of the gods. I appeal to them for justice!"

His head dropped back on to the ground, a low groan came from his lips, and then they were still, for the long sleep of death was upon him.

Nevertheless, Achilles, who was still stooping over his recumbent foe, continued to speak with rage, as if Hector could still hear him: "I know my fate," he said, "and I am resigned to it, since Patrocles has at last been avenged."

The Greeks had gathered round the corpse of their greatest enemy and were exultant. They burned with the desire to attack Troy, from which voices were raised in loud lamentation. However, Achilles had ordered his men to tie the feet of Hector to his chariot, and then the Greek champion turned his eyes towards the mourning city.

"Doubtless," he said, "the Trojans are overwhelmed by the death of their greatest hero, and it would be easy to storm their defences, but the body of Patrocles awaits burial with full honours. Let us return to the camp and sing hymns to his glory."

Voices were raised in triumph and the columns set off in battle order, cheering the victory of Achilles, who stood up in his chariot with his head proudly raised beneath the splendour of his glittering plumed helmet.

Not far away in the city, King Priam was wringing his hands and uttering loud cries of sorrow, whilst Andromache, the well-beloved wife of Hector, lay lifeless on the flagstones.

7

The Sorrows of a Father

TROY echoed with mournful cries. Preparations were being made for the funeral of Patrocles.

Achilles had forgotten already the triumph of victory and was giving himself up entirely to his sorrow.

"We must mourn Patrocles," he said to the Greeks as they returned to their tents. "And we must see to it that full tribute is paid to his remains." Thus, they conducted the funeral with pomp.

Thrice did each of the kings drive in his chariot round the bed on which lay the body of Patrocles, then sadly did the whole army file by. As for the Thessalians, they shared fully the grief of their King and in their motionless ranks they formed the last guard of honour to the dead man.

Achilles had thrown the body of Hector, face down-wards, near to the funeral litter. Then, weeping, he turned towards the remains of his friend.

"Patrocles," he said, "you see I have avenged you. The corpse of your murderer is there in the dust. Twelve young Trojans are standing by in chains, waiting to be slaughtered in honour of your funeral." The pyre had been raised near the seashore and the body of Patrocles on his funeral litter had been placed upon it.

Achilles, cup in hand, poured out libations to Zephyrus and Boreas, praying to these gods of the winds to come and fan the fire destined to burn the remains of Patrocles. Immediately there was a breeze, the fire began to crackle and, in the darkness of the night, the flames rose into the sky.

All night long Achilles stood, cup in hand, drawing wine from a golden jar and pouring it on to the crackling wood; all night his thoughts turned to his lost friend.

In the morning, when the sun began to gild the rippling waters of the sea, overwhelmed with sorrow and weari-ness, he collapsed on to the ground and for more than an hour his grief was forgotten in sleep. Then the Greek leaders came to wake him. They had come at the head of their men to pour wine over the pyre, and they gathered up the bones, placed them in a golden urn and bore them to the tent of Achilles.

Whilst the grave was being dug, funeral games were organised. Achilles took no part in them, for it was he who had to distribute the prizes to the victors. There were chariot races, wrestling matches, running races, jumping contests, javelin- and discus-throwing, sports

beloved of all the Greeks. The winners received, as rewards, slaves, fiery horses, talents of gold, precious jars or
weapons. Even the mighty Agamemnon did not scorn to
measure his skill as an archer against Meriones. Achilles
presided calmly over these games, mastering his sorrow
for a while.

But, as soon as the others had departed, and he was
alone once more in his tent, he was overcome by grief.
His mind dwelt with sad regret on the work, the pleas-
ures and the battles shared with Patrocles since his early
childhood.

"O gods of Olympus," he muttered to himself, pressing his hand against his head, "how can I allay my
hatred for the man who killed him?"

Leaping to his feet, he harnessed his horses to his
chariot and tied the body of Hector to the back of it. At
full gallop he drove thrice around the tomb of Patrocles,
his heart still filled with a mad desire for vengeance.

High up in Olympus the gods watched him and were
saddened by this spectacle. Assuredly Hector's great
courage did not deserve such shameful treatment, so
Jupiter inspired old Priam with a firm resolve to put the
matter right.

"Friends," said the old King, suddenly raising his white
head, "let us mourn no more, for our vain tears cannot
bring peace to Hector's wandering spirit. I intend to
drive down to the Greek vessels, to the tent of Achilles, to
buy back the body of my son. It is only when I see the
smoke rising from his funeral pyre that my heart will find
relief, for until that has happened my beloved Hector will
not be able to find rest in the Kingdom of the Dead. No,

Hecuba, do not prevent me from carrying out this plan. What have I to fear? That Achilles should thrust his sword through my body? I could even wish that, for I would then be able to rejoin my son."

In vain did Hecuba and his children try to restrain the old man, but a mighty will sustained him and strengthened his determination. He opened the coffers of his treasure house and drew from them his most precious possessions: splendid veils, jewels and jars of gold. All these he loaded upon his chariot, urging on his sons and his servants to act with speed.

"Father," said one of his sons timidly, "allow me to accompany you, or at least to serve as your herald?"

"No," said Priam harshly. "I wish to go alone." Then, holding up his hands in prayer towards heaven, he cried: "Oh, Jupiter, you who command the universe, deign to move the pity of Achilles on my behalf. Furthermore, to reassure this sorrowful mother by my side, grant that your eagle, king of the air and faithful interpreter of your will, may show himself at my right hand even as I pray to you?"

Scarcely had Priam spoken these words, when there was a loud rustling of feathers and, before the astonished eyes of the onlookers, a huge eagle with widespread wings suddenly descended from the depths of the sky and soared above the town on the right hand of the monarch. Hecuba gave a cry of hope.

"Dear husband," she said, helping the old man to climb into his chariot. "I have no fear now, for Jupiter has spoken. Go, and with all speed!"

Urged forward, Priam's horses bore away his chariot

at a headlong gallop. "Faster, faster," cried Priam, for whom this mad pace was still too slow.

Soon the camp of the Greeks was in sight. But how could he hope to penetrate it without being challenged at every post by the soldiers on guard? Who would lead him to the tent of Achilles? However, Jupiter did not forsake this heartbroken father. His messenger, Mercury, assumed the features of one of the slaves of the Greek champion.

"Reassure yourself," he said to the old man. "I can guide you wherever you desire."

Priam drove on without hindrance, for the god had made certain that all the guards of the camp were wrapped in sleep. Night had fallen, so Mercury skilfully steered the King of Troy through the groups of slumbering Greeks until they reached the tent of Achilles.

The hero was sitting sadly, surrounded by a group of his warriors and looking fixedly into space. Suddenly he started. This old man who staggered in, threw himself at his feet and embraced his knees, who could he be? Astonished, Achilles sat up wishing to thrust back this suppliant whose face he now recognised, but Priam would not allow himself to be driven away.

"Achilles, Achilles," he said in a voice so full of despair and sorrow that it aroused pity in the heart of the Thessalian warriors. "Hero beloved of the gods, remember your own father, who is as old as I am, and, like me, is on the threshold of the tomb. Of all the sons that I have lost in this war, Hector was the most valiant and dearly beloved of them all. Achilles, you killed him. Now give me back his body. To obtain it, I will give you all these treasures. Take pity on my old age and remember what is due to the gods."

There was a long pause, for all the Greeks were filled with compassion for the sorrows of this venerable and noble father.

"Arise, Priam," said Achilles finally, urging the old man to take a seat by his side. "My father, like you, will know the grief of losing the mainstay of his old age. Alas, I killed your son, but one of your sons will kill me and bring sorrow to my father. What else can we do? We cannot resist the laws of Destiny. We must obey the gods.

"Nevertheless, I will hearken to your plea. I will give you this body which you have come to bear away." Then, turning towards his servants, he ordered his slaves to wash the remains of Hector, to pour over them oil and balm and to clothe his body in the finest of purple tunics. Then, placed upon a funeral litter, he ordered it to be carried to the chariot of the King of Ilium.

"Priam," he continued, setting food and wine before the old man, "you must restore your strength, and then you shall sleep on a bed in my tent. I will wake you before dawn so that you may leave the camp and return to your city in safety. If Agamemnon knew of your presence here, he would perhaps wish to take back this body which I am returning to you. Tell me, O King, how many days will you give up to the funeral ceremony of Hector? So long as you will be occupied in this sad duty, so long shall I prevent the Greeks from attacking your city."

Tremulously Priam kissed the hands of Achilles. "Great hero," he said, stammering with joy. "How generous you are to give me time to mourn my son undisturbed! I tell you now that in twelve days the Trojans will be ready to take up arms once more."

A few hours later the Trojan King's chariot passed through the ancient gate of the city amidst the cries of welcome and tears of sorrow of all his people. Over the whole sad scene of mourning and desolation dawn cast her warming glow.

PART TWO

THE ODYSSEY

Introduction

The *Odyssey* is the story of the wanderings of Ulysses—also called Odysseus—after the fall of Troy.

The Greek leaders quarrelled over the plunder, and so they set off in different directions.

Ulysses was King of Ithaca, a small island off the west coast of Greece, but he took ten years to return to his own land because the gods from above were divided about him. Some supported him and others hindered his progress.

He had a great many adventures: he was nearly killed by the giant, Polyphemus, and he narrowly escaped being turned into a pig by the sorceress, Circe.

Then he was detained on an island for eight years by the nymph, Calypso, who offered him immortality and perpetual youth if he would stay. But in his heart he longed to return to Ithaca, where his wife and his son were waiting for him with great anxiety.

The story closes when Ulysses comes back to Ithaca disguised as a beggar and succeeds in dealing with the forty suitors who were pestering his wife, Penelope, insisting that she should choose one of them as a husband.

I

The Sorrows of a Queen

USE, sing to me of this hero, famed for his cunning, who set forth on his endless wanderings after having destroyed the walls of holy Troy. Dauntlessly he strove against the direst of perils, and even against the stern will of the Olympian gods themselves. Muse, sing to me of this valiant mortal who by his perseverance overcame the harsh decrees of Destiny.

Ten years had passed since the fall of Troy, and all the survivors of this epic siege had returned to their homes, with only one exception. The palace of Ulysses, King of Ithaca, had no master, and the kingdom which he had ruled so wisely and so well was torn by dissensions between the suitors for the hand of his wife, Penelope, though his son, Telemachus, was of age.

Proud as he was, and with all the energy of youth, the young man was longing to save Ithaca from the greed of those who were bringing about her ruin, but what could he accomplish alone against so many rivals? The people who had submitted joyfully to Ulysses, their chosen chief, did not support Telemachus, who seemed to them too young and too submissive to his mother.

"Surely," they said, "a stripling who can stand by and watch a lot of intruders squandering his wealth is not the King for us." In these circumstances, it was not to be wondered at that Ithaca was gradually being ruined.

However, despite all these difficulties, the fact that Telemachus did preserve some degree of independence was due to a woman, and that woman was his mother.

Penelope, wife of Ulysses, refused to believe that her husband was dead. She knew that he had not been killed during the siege of Troy. She knew also that he was the real conqueror of that almost impregnable city, and that his wisdom and cunning had succeeded where Achilles, Ajax and Agamemnon had failed. So she could not believe that this hero of whom she was so proud could have succumbed in a mere tempest.

Therefore, she trembled with anger and grief when she heard the voices of the intruders in her palace, laughing, singing and feasting so loudly that the sound penetrated to the women's quarters. She was even more indignant because each of these upstarts wanted to marry her, in order to become King of Ithaca, for the husband of the widow of Ulysses would occupy his throne. Such was the law, and indeed Penelope was obliged to accept its ruling.

In truth, she was filled with horror at the idea of becoming the wife of any of these tiresome intruders, but, using her feminine guile, she found a way out of her dilemma by pretending to agree to this course. "But," she added when making this statement, "I must first of all complete the tapestry which I intend to offer up to the goddess Minerva. It would be blasphemy not to carry out my promise."

When the impatient suitors asked her how long it would take, she replied that she spent most of her time at her loom. This was, indeed, true, but the cunning queen did not explain that she spent half the night unravelling the work she had woven during the day.

The suitors had to wait, not only for months, but for years. So the patience and loyalty of a weak woman inspired her to outwit the ambition of a number of greedy and unscrupulous men.

"O gods," sighed Penelope, worn out with long years of waiting. "Take pity on us, for we are almost defenceless."

Nevertheless, her prayers had not been in vain. At the time when her suitors were wont to gather and play at dice in the Great Hall of the palace, a tall man of noble bearing appeared on the threshold. From his grey hairs and sober dress, it would seem that he was an elderly merchant who had come to Ithaca to sell his merchandise, but his eyes burnt with a divine fire. It was Minerva, goddess of the mind and protectress of the wise Ulysses, who had been granted leave by Jupiter to disguise herself and bring consolation to those who mourned the hero.

On seeing a newcomer, Telemachus went up to greet the stranger.

8

"Welcome," he said. "Enter and accept the hospitality of my palace. When you have rested, you shall tell me what has brought you here. I have many questions to ask of you, for whenever a traveller visits this island, I hope to have news of my father."

During the banquet and feasting that followed, Telemachus continued to interrogate his guest. He spoke in whispers for fear of being overheard by the suitors, but he could not conceal his sorrow and anxiety. "I always hope that every newcomer will bring me news of my father, but no one can tell me where he is."

"Why despair?" replied Minerva. "Can it not be that your father is the prisoner of wild men on some distant isle? You must be Telemachus, and the father whose fate perturbs you is assuredly Ulysses, King of Ithaca."

"That is so," sighed the young man, "but who may you be, stranger?"

"My name is of no account. All that concerns you is that I am a friend of Ulysses, and that I am interested to bring you word of this. Now I pray you, what is the cause of all this feasting? Is this a wedding or a banquet? Why so much rejoicing and extravagance when the master of the house is far away?"

"My father's absence and our anxiety on his behalf are not our only grounds for sorrow," said Telemachus, overwhelmed with grief. "The island chieftains vie with each other for my mother's hand, and as she postpones acceptance, they consume my heritage in feasting here. Would to heaven that Ulysses were here to deal with them with his javelins. All this talk of marriage would end in mourning."

"Now, pay heed to me," said Minerva, rising. "To-morrow, summon these chiefs to Council, and bid them return to their abodes. Then prepare a ship with twenty oarsmen, seek out your father's friends—kings such as noble Nestor and amber-haired Menelaus, who battled by his side in the long siege of Troy. From these you may learn that he still lives. If he is no more, then shall you come back to Ithaca and rid your palace of these suitors who importune you so. Have you not heard how Orestes killed his father's murderer? Be courageous as he was, and gain as much renown. And now, farewell, for I must depart to my ship and leave you."

"Stranger," the young man replied. "You have my gratitude, but bide with me still, for your presence gives me courage."

But as he spoke the goddess vanished as swiftly as any eagle on the wing.

"Assuredly," cried Telemachus, "no mortal could fade from before my eyes with such speed? It must be Minerva herself who came to guide me with her wisdom, for I feel within my heart a wondrous change."

Antinous, boldest and vilest of all his mother's suitors, then spoke to him. "What did the stranger want of you and why did he leave so soon? Did he perchance announce your father's coming?" he sneered with mocking laughter.

With bolder bearing, Telemachus then addressed the suitors:

"To-morrow," he said, firmly, "we must all meet in Council, so that I may speak to the assembled people."

Then he walked majestically through the ranks of the

rival suitors to retire to his own lofty chamber, among the tall cypresses of the palace gardens.

"Wise Euryclea," he said to his old nurse, who had come forward to greet him. "I wish to speak to you alone, for you did nurture me. Since you enjoyed my father's trust, you can guide me in my designs. Keep well my secret, for were it known I could not leave this isle."

"O heavens," lamented Euryclea. "Must you venture thus alone on to the stormy seas? Is it not enough that Ulysses should have perished far away from the land that bred him? What am I to say to old Laertes, your grandfather, if he should ask, 'Where is the prince we left in your care?'"

"Calm your fears," said Telemachus consolingly. "I would not go if the gods had not decreed it. Swear now to conceal my departure from my mother and all the suitors that beset her."

Since Euryclea could refuse nothing to the child that she had nursed, she took a solemn oath to keep his secret.

"It is well," continued Telemachus. "Though I can now count on your silence, I also need your help. Since you have kept my father's storehouse, take twenty measures of the finest flour and put it in stout goatskins; fill twelve urns with the best wine, so that I may have supplies for my journey. Do this swiftly and secretly, for I must depart to-morrow at nightfall."

*　　　　　*　　　　　*

Just as crimson dawn tinged the eastern sky, Telemachus sprang from his couch and charged the heralds to summon all citizens, in the King's name, to assemble; then, with firm step, he strode into the city square before the admiring crowd.

"Who, then, has called us to Council?" asked the elders, "and for what purpose? But we must listen, for the time for meeting is long due."

So majestic was his gait, so stern his face, that for the first time the people felt that Telemachus was the true son of Ulysses, and gave way to him respectfully as he walked up the steps to his father's throne.

"Listen to me, men of Ithaca. It is the first time that I have spoken to you since great Ulysses left these shores. I cannot, alas, give you tidings of his return, nor even treat of our common weal, since I must talk to you of myself alone and of the misfortunes that beset my home and family. Soon I may bewail the ruin of my house, see my patrimony laid waste, for greedy chieftains would wed my mother against her wish. They dare not seek consent from Icarus, her father, who alone can dispose of her hand, and of the heritage which should be my portion. Moreover, these intruders have chosen to remain within my palace, consuming in their feasting my sheep, my goats, my cattle and my choicest wines, without restraint. Too young, too weak and unsupported, I cannot alone re-dress this evil nor drive away these wicked men. Citizens, in honour of my father's memory, grant me your help to save his spouse from shame and abuse. Since you are here to judge my wrongs, are you my friends or do you side with my oppressors?"

Rising quickly, Antinous thus replied:

"So, young cub, you would make us odious with your

high-sounding speeches, but the offence lies not with us alone. Has not your mother, with her cunning, deceived us all for four long years? So long as she outwits us and refuses to make her choice, so long will we remain in your palace. So much the worse for you, if you cannot order her to go."

"Antinous," cried Telemachus, enraged. "So you would have me cast my mother out and incur the hatred of all men? Those words I never will pronounce. Go! Depart yourselves, before I summon all the gods to avenge me."

And while he spake with arms upraised, two eagles from the mountain-top swooped down with outstretched wings above the assembled Greeks. Three times they wheeled, eyeing the crowd with ominous look, then soared upwards into the sky.

"An evil presage," cried some in awe, and then the ancient seer, Halitherses, famed for his prophecies, declared:

"Men of Ithaca, lend me your ears, for dangers threaten all, but threaten even more the suitors. Ere Ulysses set forth for Troy, I foretold to him that, after many trials and endless losses, he alone would return when twenty years had passed. These years are sped, and thus, before long, Ulysses will appear before us."

"Old fool," replied Eurymachus, roughest of all the suitors, shrugging his shoulders. "Who cares for the flutterings of these wild birds, and which of us could find predictions in them? I can foretell that if you persist in these foolish stories, peril will befall you from our hands. As for Telemachus, let him urge his mother to her father's house, that he may force her to choose a suitor. What say you of my prediction?" he added, turning to the crowd of suitors.

"It is well said," they cried in unison.

"Heed me, chieftains," quoth Mentor, friend of wise Ulysses. "Blindly, you run to your destruction, and you, men of Ithaca, may indeed share their fate, for by your craven silence you have not curbed their greed and boldness. Why should Ulysses spare you on his return? Why should kings show mercy to those whom they have ruled and protected who yet have displayed no gratitude?" Then, going to Telemachus, he added:

"And what action will you take, O Prince?"

"I sail to-day for Pylos and Sparta to seek news of my father," replied the Prince.

"Would that I could go with you," said Mentor, "for you will prove your worth and show your father's courage. Take no heed of the suitors' projects, for they will soon learn that all their plans must come to naught."

"Telemachus," said Antinous with a smile, "be not overbold. Join us in our feasting. Then will I soon forget the harsh words you spoke against us."

But Telemachus replied: "I have no heart for feasting with guests so insolent, nor can I forget the wrongs that your friends have done me. . . ."

"Let him be, Antinous," spoke Leocritus, another suitor. "Who knows if he will not perish in a storm, like Ulysses, his father, and never return to Ithaca?"

2

With the Conquerors of Troy

OW down on the horizon, the sun was emerging from the rippling waves as Telemachus and his crew arrived in the port of Pylos. The dwellers of the nine cities of Nestor's realm were assembled on the beach to offer up to great Neptune, lord of the widespread seas, a sacrifice of nine sable bulls.

Telemachus sprang ashore, followed, it seemed, by Mentor, though such was the radiance of his gaze and the majesty of his gait that perchance it was Minerva who bore his shape to conceal her presence there.

"Telemachus," he said, "forget your fears, for there is no longer cause for them. Did you not cross the sea to discover what country is concealing your father? Can you not allow the aged Nestor to guide you with his wise advice?"

Thus encouraged, Telemachus advanced with firm tread to greet the old man.

"Strangers," said Pisistratus, the youngest of the King's sons, "be welcome here," and, taking both by the hand, placed them beside the festive table. "Here do we celebrate the Ocean King's great day. Before you drink this wine, pour our libations to him, for this is the homage we owe the gods."

Taking the proffered cup, Mentor gave thanks to Neptune for having guided them safely into port.

"Great god," he said in moving tones, "listen to our supplications, we beseech you. Bless those who welcome us here, and grant that Telemachus and I may succeed in all our wishes and return home in safety."

"Whence come you, strangers?" said Nestor with surprise. "And who may you be?"

"O son of Neleus, wisest of ancient kings. We come from the shady groves of Ithaca, and I am the son of that Ulysses who, with your aid, conquered Troy's holy city."

"Young friend and son of my dearest friend. I see in you his features, and when you speak I hear his voice. Has he not returned to his kingdom?"

"Alas, no," replied the young man with sadness. "No man knows what has befallen him or if he may have met his death at sea. His fate alone is hidden of all the Greeks who fought at Troy. Brave Achilles was killed by Paris, Ajax was drowned when sailing home, Agamemnon was murdered on his return to Mycenae. But what of my father? Where can he be? I implore you, sage Nestor, tell me if you can bring to mind aught that he said or did which might guide me to the truth. Then may I know if all my hopes be in vain."

"Dear son, what may I say to you?" sighed Nestor. "So little do I know of your brave father's fate. When Troy fell, we Greeks shared her captives and her treasures and by our dissensions provoked the gods to anger. Did not our leaders summon us to council when the sun's full course was sped, and so offend them, for night was made for slumber? Despite my efforts to dissuade him from this course, Lord Agamemnon persisted in it, for Destiny had sealed his fate. Throughout the night we discoursed with anger. When morning came, Diomedes, Menelaus, Ulysses and myself embarked with half the Grecian host, whilst Agamemnon remained on the Asian shore with the other half. Near Tenedos we parted from Ithaca's fleet, whilst Menelaus found haven at Lesbos.

"Our sacrifices made to Neptune brought favouring winds to Diomedes and me, and in four days I sailed to Pylos, and he to Argos. I have learned since that Pyrrhus, son of proud Achilles, made safe return to Grecian shores, as did Philoctetus and Idomeneus.

"As for brave Menelaus, a sudden tempest overwhelmed full half his ships. Forced by the winds to distant Egypt, seven long years passed before he came safe to Mycenae, only to witness the funeral of his dead brother, Agamemnon's murderer, whom Orestes had slaughtered in revenge. In his long wanderings, Menelaus may well have heard news of your father's fate."

"My intention was to seek him out in Sparta, after paying homage to you, O glorious Nestor," replied Telemachus with great respect. "Thus, if you will allow it, I will no longer accept your hospitality, but will sail on, for now the winds are favourable."

"No," said Mentor with the authority of the mouth-piece of Minerva. "Stay here this night with Nestor, Telemachus, for you must not strain so soon great Neptune's kindness. To-morrow Pisistrates will take you in his chariot as far as Sparta."

"A wise counsel," quoth Nestor, taking Telemachus by the hand. "Stay with me in my palace, and rest from your journey."

But Mentor would not accept this offer and, claiming that he was called to a neighbouring city and taking leave of his host, he vanished so swiftly that those who stood by were filled with amazement.

"Young man," said Nestor pensively, "if I am not deceived, your friend is only a semblance of a mortal, for I believe that this Mentor who brought you here is none other than great Jove's daughter, the invincible Minerva, in disguise.

"O mighty goddess, who came within our midst," prayed the aged King, "be favourable to our endeavours. Grant us your support, I beg, and I will offer up to you a milk-white heifer which has never bowed down under the yoke of man."

The next day at dawn, Telemachus stepped into Nestor's chariot, which was drawn by the swiftest horses in the old man's stables and driven by Pisistratus. A good store of provisions had been prepared for the voyagers, as the journey to Sparta was a long one.

Then after the right and seemly sacrifice had been offered up to Minerva to preserve the travellers from the perils of the road, the two young men set off at a full gallop, leaving behind them long clouds of dust stirred up by their chariot wheels and by their horses' hooves.

Night was falling when, two days later, they first saw the great towers of Sparta in the far distance. As they drew nearer, they heard the sound of feasting, of singing, and of the clash of cymbals. Filled with astonishment, they asked a peasant the reason for all this rejoicing.

"This day," was the answer, "the son and the daughter of our King are to be married. The fair Hermione is to wed Pyrrhus, the glorious son of Achilles, and the worthy Megapeuthus is to take as his bride a maiden of Sparta. Nothing can be more splendid than the dancing and music in the palace to celebrate this double event."

"What are we to do?" said Telemachus to Pisistratus. "How can we dare disturb the happiness of this moment with the sad problems of my quest?"

"You may be right," said Pisistratus, "but it would be slighting to Menelaus if we displayed any doubts about the generosity of his hospitality. He would wish to be most lavish, even were he not a close friend of your father. Furthermore, did he not learrn to appreciate the hospitality of many a host during his seven years of unceasing wandering? We may go in without any hesitation."

Pisistratus spoke truly. Even before he learned the names of his guests, Menelaus greeted them with the greatest warmth and cordiality. Baths were prepared that they might wash away the dust of the highway: slaves rubbed them down with scented oil. The travellers were given richly embroidered tunics of the finest weave, and led into the hall, where Menelaus sat in the company of the newly-wedded couples. When his guests approached, the King received them with outstretched hands and beckoned them to sit down by his side.

"You must share in our rejoicings," he said, "and when you have rested and taken refreshment, you must tell me the full aim and purpose of your visit to me. Slaves," he shouted, "bring in the finest cuts of meat, and fill these golden cups with the best wine from our cellars. I myself will wait upon the new friends whom the hand of Fate has guided to the gates of my palace."

And, turning towards Telemachus, he placed before him the portion always allotted to kings: the shin of an ox delicately roasted to a golden brown, and dripping with rich gravy.

"My thanks to you, O King," murmured Telemachus, moved by this last expression of friendship. "I cannot tell you of my joy in being welcomed into so splendid a palace by so great a monarch. My dear Pisistratus," he added, turning to his companion who, like himself, was filled with admiration for the luxury that surrounded them, "might we not be in the great hall of Olympus, where Jupiter sits enthroned in the midst of all the Immortals? Behold these rich carpets, these heavily embroidered hangings and all these most precious objects. Their ivory, amber, silver, bronze and gold combine to present a mosaic of brilliance and colour. Never could I have imagined that such astounding beauty could, in truth, exist. What delight and what joy it must be to dwell in the midst of such treasures!"

Menelaus smiled sadly at this outburst of admiration.

"If I told you, my son, that I am far from happy, would you believe me?"

Then, gazing into the distance and as if speaking to himself, the King continued:

"There can be no greater bitterness than to be surrounded by all these riches, and to realise that it is through me that so many heroes who loved life and its joys have become mere shadows in the Kingdom of the Dead. Sometimes, when my hand strays over the purple folds of fine linens, it is as if I beheld a flow of blood trickling between my fingers. Indeed, my palace is filled with the treasures of Troy, my barns are bursting with piled-up grain, my stables are not large enough to hold all my horses and cattle, but often I seem to hear cries of pain and of anguish in the midst of which I seem to discern the voices of much-loved friends, whom I shall see no more except in memory. My brother has been murdered, Ajax, too, has gone, whilst the loss of Ulysses, my dearest friend, weighs every year more heavily upon my heart. Ah, would to heaven that I had stayed at home in poverty, rather than be enriched by spoils such as these. Had I not set out for Troy, how many heroes who died for the honour of Greece would still be alive to-day!"

On hearing the name of his father pronounced, Telemachus could not refrain from weeping.

"What ails you, young man?" asked Menelaus quickly. "Can my sorrow afflict you so sorely? Why these tears?"

"Noble Menelaus," replied Pisistratus, "you see before you the son of this Ulysses whom you mourn so deeply. My father, Nestor, King of Pylos, charged me to bring him to you here, to ask for your aid and counsel. Not only has Telemachus not seen his father again, but his life in Ithaca is made unbearable by the presence of hostile oppressors."

On hearing these words, Menelaus embraced the two young men, delighted to find that they resembled their fathers in many features.

"Ah," remarked the King to Telemachus, "how many times did I speak of the future with my dear Ulysses, saying: 'If we shall ever return from Troy, we must not again be parted or separated from each other. You shall leave your island of Ithaca with all your people and shall take up your dwelling in one of the cities near Sparta. You shall choose whatever pleases you best, and I will give you full possession of it, building for you also a palace worthy of your rank and of our friendship. Yet the sea has carried him far away from me, this hero, the wisest of all the Greeks and the true conqueror of Troy. The gods, jealous of our promised happiness, have prevented this unfortunate man alone from returning home."

Tears welled up in the eyes of Menelaus as he pronounced these words, and he sighed deeply.

"Come," he continued, placing an arm round the shoulders of Telemachus, "you are here to seek my help, and I only add to your sadness. It is late. May the dark veils of night take away our afflictions. To-morrow we will continue our discourse."

At a sign from the King, slaves led away the two young men to the great porch of the palace, where had been prepared for them a soft couch of furs with blankets of silky wool. Soon Telemachus and Pisistratus laid aside their sorrows and their weariness and their minds strayed into the wondrous land of dreams.

*   *   *

Soon after the dawn of the next day, the King sought out Telemachus, and spoke to him with great affection: "Dear son," he said, "tell me about the purpose of your journey. You may trust me as you would your own father."

Telemachus spoke of the threatening insolence of his mother's suitors, and of the havoc that they were making of the royal palace of Ithaca. Then he besought Menelaus to tell him all that he knew about Ulysses, declaring that he would even prefer a cruel certainty rather than have to endure so long a suspense.

Menelaus listened indignantly to the account of the way in which the citizens of Ithaca had insulted the memory of their King.

"So," he said, "when the lion is away the hyenas come and despoil his lair, without realising in their folly that the king of beasts may well return. He will come back, and then all these wanton braggarts will be cast into the eternal shadows of the tomb. Ulysses is not dead. Of this I am sure, for I believe the words of Proteus, whose kingdom is in the bed of the salt sea, deep below the rippling waves. This is what his prophecy did reveal to me. But ere I tell you of it, you must hear my story! My ships had been scattered by wind and I was driven by gales to the coast of Egypt, where I was long detained as a captive. One day, in an attempt to make my escape, I landed in a

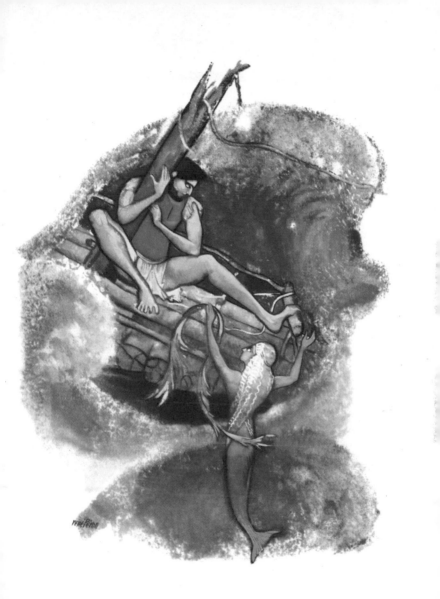

" Bind this scarf around your breast"

creek off the north coast of the isle of Pharos. Though water was plentiful, we soon lacked food, and so we fished, but in vain, for we could catch nothing. I was overwhelmed with despair when the nereid, Idothea, was moved by our sufferings.

"She told me that her father, Proteus, could reveal to me the reason for our misfortunes, and the fact that they were soon to come to an end. She added, also, that he would tell me of the fate of the companions whose loss I was bewailing.

"Revived by this thought, I turned to the beautiful goddess and said: 'But how shall I dare to come nigh to the immortal Proteus, divine shepherd of the flocks of Neptune? Will he not turn into a fleck of foam as soon as he sees me approach?'

"'No,' replied the nereid. 'All you need do is to bind him with chains and keep him by your side to make him do your will. Hearken to me now: He comes every evening with his herd of seals to sleep in one of the grottoes of this island. So you and three of your picked men should wrap yourselves up in sealskins, and thus disguised you may approach him. As soon as he falls asleep, bind him up. Be assured, you have nought to fear from him. Then you may question him and find out all about the future which torments you so.'

"I followed this advice, and our wiles succeeded. A few hours later Proteus lay at my feet loaded with chains.

"'Venerable old man,' I said to him, 'I would hear the truth about my future. When shall I see my country again, the land where I was born? What has become of

9

all the heroes so dear to me? What of Agamemnon, Ajax and Ulysses?'

"Then, my dear son, Proteus told me that, so long as I had not made sacrifices on the banks of the Nile to appease the gods of Olympus, so long would I be unable to return to Sparta. He told me how my brother, Agamemnon, had been vilely murdered, how Ajax had been drowned in a storm. Then he added:

"'You wish to know what has become of Ulysses? He is held in bondage by the nymph, Calypso. When I beheld him last, the tears were streaming down his face as he looked at the waves that lashed the reefs of the island, for he has neither vessel nor ship to bear him back to his native land.'

"Dear son," continued Menelaus, "that is all that I know, for I am sure that the god told me the truth. If Ulysses can escape from captivity, he will assuredly return and drive away from his palace these loathsome intruders who are oppressing his wife and his son. But who can tell when that time will be?

"In the meantime, it is my wish that you stay with me, and I will give you my finest chariot and my swiftest horses, a palace to live in, herds of plump sheep and fields for them to graze in."

Telemachus shook his head sadly.

"Bountiful Menelaus," he replied, "I must leave you now that I know the answer to my quest. Even though Ithaca may be the most barren of our islands, I love it, for is it not the land of my birth?"

"Since that is so," replied Menelaus, "you shall have all the gifts that you can bear away. Let us now offer a sacrifice to safeguard your departure, for who knows if Ulysses himself will be on your native shores to welcome you?"

But whilst festivities were being prepared in honour of Telemachus in Sparta, activities of a different kind were taking place in the palace of Ulysses in Ithaca.

When Penelope's suitors were told of the departure of Telemachus, they began to fear that ere long he would return with his father.

"We must see to it that he does not come back," said Leocritus. "Let us conceal ourselves on the islet of Asteria, for there on one side a creek faces Ithaca. When the young man's ship passes, we will attack it from behind, so that he cannot escape. Our own craft is a strong one, we have stout oarsmen, and so it will be a light task to dispose of so inexperienced a seaman."

This suggestion was greeted with loud applause, and as soon as the red sun had disappeared over the horizon the suitors set off to prepare their ambush.

As it happened, Penelope had witnessed their departure from the roof of her palace, and her heart was filled with anxiety, though she knew not why.

Suddenly she heard the loud tread of running feet behind her. It was Medon, an old servant of Ulysses, who stood before her, trembling, and with water dripping from his clothes.

"O Queen," he stammered, "I have made my escape from yonder ship to warn you of the danger that threatens you. Leocritus and Antinous are on board, and they are lying in wait for the return of Prince Telemachus, with the intention of killing him."

"His return?" said Penelope, in surprise. "Euryclea told me that my son had stayed at home and would see no one."

"It is not so, O Queen," replied Medon. "The Prince set off for Pylos and for Sparta to seek news of our King. This took place a few days ago. I was told that Mentor had gone with him, but this must be an error, for I saw Mentor this morning in the city square."

On hearing these words, Penelope ran downstairs and sped towards the palace of Telemachus, where she encountered Euryclea.

"My son?" cried Penelope. "Where is my son? You have delivered him up to be assassinated by these vile intruders."

"Beloved mistress," said Euryclea, weeping. "Kill me if you wish, but I only obeyed the orders of the Prince, my master, because of my love for him. He may yet be saved, and so let us call upon Minerva, daughter of great Jupiter, to protect him. She will give you back your son, even were he on the brink of the Kingdom of the Dead."

Then, putting on her finest garments, the old nurse went up to the terrace of the palace, followed by all the other women slaves. With trembling hands, Euryclea raised towards heaven a basketful of consecrated barley and began to pray:

"O invincible daughter of the mighty King of Olympus, O Minerva, protect the son of our hero."

3

Nausicaa of the Milk White Arms

ALYPSO, the beautiful nymph, still held Ulysses in thrall whilst these events were taking place in Ithaca. The hero who was being mourned there and was awaited with such despair was also grieving and distraught as he wept in the far-away island where he was held captive.

He found no relief in the delights around him: the cool grotto and the nearby forest where the birds sang unceasingly; the fountains and the brooks in which flowed clear, sparkling water; the vines laden with golden grapes and the turf spangled with flowers of all colours. The gods themselves could not have passed through these glades without falling under the spell of their enchantment.

Nevertheless, Ulysses lay on the shore and watched the waves with staring eyes and sorrow in his heart.

"The sea is a barrier," he murmured, "more impenetrable than all the mountains of the world together. Is it to separate me for ever from my son, my wife and my native land?"

"Ulysses," said a gentle voice behind him suddenly.

Calypso had come nigh to her captive, and placed her hand on his massive brow, which was racked with grief.

Then, with a sigh, she began to speak:

"Put aside the grief that consumes your heart, for the King of the gods has given leave for your departure and I must obey. Therefore, ungrateful man, you may depart from hence. Had you stayed, I would have given you immortality and you could have dwelt for ever in this island of eternal summer. Since you weep for your barren land and your white-haired spouse, I will help you. Fell these great oak trees to make yourself a boat large enough to bear you across the seas, and I will give you water, stores of wheat and of wine as well as clothes; moreover, I will ask Aeolus, god of the winds, to speed you on with favourable breezes. Do not gaze at me with distrust. Do you, in truth, believe that I would avenge your indifference? No; I swear by the great Styx which flows through the Kingdom of the Dead that I have only one wish, and that is to witness your departure."

Taking up the axe which the nymph had brought him, Ulysses set to work and felled one tree after another. Swiftly, he trimmed them and shaped them into beams, and in four days his task was accomplished and the craft had a tiller, a mast, sails and ropes when he launched it into the sea.

Since the weather was fair and the breezes blew softly,

Ulysses set sail, and swiftly his boat skimmed over the lapping waves.

For seventeen days the hero journeyed on without mishap. On the far horizon, the wooded hills of the Phaeacians were beginning to loom up against the sky when Neptune rose above the waves. Remembering past slights, his anger grew. "Behold, a loathsome Greek," he roared in anger. Spreading thick clouds on land and sea at his bequest, the winds began to blow furiously, raising up waves of enormous height. Ulysses grew pale and sighed.

"Alas!" he said. "I am accursed of the gods. Why did I not meet my death like so many other Greeks on the plains of Troy? I should have been buried with great honour, and my name would have been inscribed next to that of the valiant Achilles, but now I shall die in obscurity and my body will be tossed about by the salt sea waves."

While he lamented thus, a huge billow suddenly wrested Ulysses from the tiller to which he clung and carried him off into the sea. Still buffeted by the waves, he swam towards his raft, but tiller, mast, sails, and stores had drifted away upon the flood, and he remained grasping the bare wreckage that was left, a prey to all the contrary winds.

For two long days the victim of driving tempests, the hero's courage never failed him, even though he could see the nereids shedding tears of pity at his plight. Great Cadmus's lovely daughter saw him and her heart was moved. Sitting athwart the raft, she addressed him thus:

"Cast off your garments, and bind this scarf around

your breast; then thrust aside your craft and swim for shore. But remember, ere you land you must cast it away with face averted."

So saying, she plunged once more into the deep, and as Ulysses sat perplexed, a huge wave struck his raft, making the timbers fly on every side like straws before a frolic wind. As swimming was now his sole resource, the hero broke through the billows once again with untiring limbs until, at last, the sea was stilled, for Neptune's wrath had waned.

"I can see land at last," the hero murmured with delight. With weariness, hunger and sleepless nights forgotten, he swam with greater zest towards the beckoning shore, for forests and hills appeared before his eyes, as did likewise the rending rocks and fearful eddies.

A huge wave heaved him towards the land, while Minerva's watchful arm guided him to the mouth of a smooth-flowing river.

Mindful of the nereid's warning, Ulysses loosed the scarf and cast it behind him without a backward glance. Then, bending low, he stooped to kiss the soil, the sacred earth, mother of every mortal.

Breathless and speechless, he lay until the fresh wind of dawn chilled his limbs.

"If I ascend yonder hillock," the hero said, "there is shelter in the grove from rough winds and savage beasts." Lying on leaves beneath boughs intertwined above him, the weary Ulysses fell asleep, finding repose and oblivion to all adversity.

But whilst he slumbered on, Minerva flew light-footed to the great city of the Phaeacians, for it was in their land that Ulysses had been washed ashore, and their King was called Alcinous.

This wise and venerable man was ever busy seeing to the needs of his subjects. His wife, the noble Arete, was descended, so it was said, from the sea-god, Neptune. Indeed, there was something godly about the proud glance and graceful gait of this beauteous Queen, and all her children resembled her. Of these, young Nausicaa was the most lovely, the most gentle princess of them all.

Minerva leant over the bed of the young girl, who slept with one of her smooth white arms flung back over her outspread golden hair; a smile of hope and happiness trembled on her lips. Her father was to marry her soon to a noble Phaeacian, and the dream of this coming wedding filled her heart with delight.

Minerva breathed on this pure brow and there came a dream into the mind of Nausicaa. It seemed to her that her dearest friend, the daughter of Dymas, was seated by her side and said to her in words of reproach:

"How idle you are, Nausicaa. See! All your finest garments, your veils, your tunics and your girdles are faded and soiled, and yet the day will soon dawn when you must appear in all your beauty in the house of your betrothed. Rise, therefore, with all haste! Ask your father for one of his chariots in which you will place all your garments and take them down to the riverside. With the help of your handmaidens, you will wash all your linen in its waters."

Nausicaa rubbed her eyes, sitting up and looking around her, but, except for her faithful hound, there was no one in her room. How foolish I am, thought the young girl. I really believed that Amyra had spoken to me. Yet it was nothing but a dream. However, there was truth in it, for this veil has lost its whiteness and this girdle its freshness. Assuredly, I must wash them in the river.

Then Nausicaa ran with nimble feet to ask her father for his help.

"Beloved father," she said, pressing his hand to her lips. "Will you not give orders that one of your great chariots be harnessed? My clothes have lost their freshness, and I would go to wash them in the river."

"Your wish is granted," said the King. "My servants will prepare the chariot forthwith."

Smiling and blushing, Nausicaa called her handmaidens and bade them place the garments in the chariot together with food and wine and precious oils that she and her companions might anoint themselves after bathing their limbs.

On reaching the river banks, the maidens unharnessed the white mules that drew the chariot to let them graze in the waterside meadows. Then they set to their task singing and laughing as they worked, and when they had washed the garments, they spread them out upon the pebbles of the shore to dry, for the sun was already high up in the heaven and its rays were full of warmth.

"Come maidens," said Nausicaa, "let us bathe. Then we will eat and frolic at leisure."

Obedient to these orders, the young girls set aside their clothing and plunged into the clear waters of the river. Then, refreshed and full of joy, they played with the ball their mistress threw them. So far did she launch it that it flew past their outstretched hands and rolled down the hillside slope. With a despairing cry, the Princess sped in pursuit of it, rousing Ulysses from his slumbers by her cries.

"What is it?" he said, startled. "Who has spoken? Who has called out? Are these nymphs from woodland, stream or meadow?" And, rising to his feet, he lifted the branches which hid him from the maidens' gaze.

When he appeared, a cry of alarm arose, and the girls, frightened by the sight of this naked man, covered with foam and sand, hid behind the shrubs on the riverside. Alone, Nausicaa remained motionless, for her soul knew no fear. She looked at Ulysses with such pride and noble bearing that the hero dared not approach.

"Goddess," he said with great respect. "Do I see in you Diana, great Jupiter's own daughter? Forgive a mortal such as I for daring to speak to you, but my misfortunes must be my plea. I have fought against storm and wave for so many days, that the mere sight of your beauty fills me with enchantment and incites me to look boldly at you. Goddess, I promise you the sacrifice of my finest horses if ever I set foot again on the soil of my fatherland."

Flattered by the homage of this stranger, whose courteous bearing proved that she was not dealing with a bold malefactor, she smiled.

"I am no immortal," said she. "My name is Nausicaa, daughter of Alcinous, King of the Phaeacian land.

"Princess," replied Ulysses. "Bear me no ill-will for my error. Who would not have taken you for a goddess? But since I have found haven in your father's realm, let me implore you to tell me the way to the city. Deign, also, to give me one of these tunics spread out on the shore, so that I may dare to approach my fellow-men. And may the gods give you the kindly husband that your mercy and beauty merit."

Nausicaa called her handmaidens and ordered them to give Ulysses clothes, food and wine, which he received with great joy. First he dived into the river before putting on the rich tunic that he was given. Then, sitting on the river bank, he ate and drank with delight.

The maidens looked at him with curiosity, admiring his great stature, the nobility of his bearing and the dark halo of hair around his face.

Whilst her maidens folded the laundered garments and placed them in the chariot, Nausicaa gently came up to Ulysses.

"Stranger," she said, "you asked me to show you the way to my father's city. All you need do is to follow me, for the sun is sinking into the sea, and I must return to the palace. You may present yourself without fear before my father, for never did Alcinous despise a prayer or send away a petitioner, but I pray you, speak also to my mother, for her advice is listened to by my father, so great is her wisdom. You will find her spinning in the porch of our palace. Tell her of your misfortunes, but do not speak of our encounter, for if we had been seen together, not only would my reputation suffer, but I should become the scorn of every tavern in the town. That is why you must fall behind as soon as we come to the fountain of Minerva, which is surrounded by a grove of poplars, for the reputation of the daughter of Alcinous must be above suspicion."

"Princess," said Ulysses, bowing to the ground. "I

would rather die than bring shame to the noblest character and the gentlest heart on earth. I will follow your directions implicitly."

Nausicaa smiled, climbed into her chariot, and drove off, with her handmaidens walking on either side, whilst Ulysses followed at a respectful distance.

"Farewell, stranger," said she as they arrived at the grove dedicated to Minerva. "May the goddess keep you under her care."

Ulysses gave thanks to his divine protectress, for he was sure that it was she who had brought Nausicaa into his life. Then encouraged, he set forth on his mission.

Passing through the gates, he crossed the city, admiring on his way the splendid ships moored in the harbour, the broad streets, and the crowds of merchants from every country that thronged the squares.

On reaching the wondrous gates of the palace, Ulysses sought out the Queen, ran up to her and threw himself at her feet, begging her to take pity on an unfortunate who had been separated for so many years from those whom he loved. Then, turning to Alcinous, he made similar petitions to him.

"Rise, stranger," said the King finally. "If I have the means of putting an end to your misfortunes, you will, before long, see your country and your family. Take your place by my side and be my guest. Since night is about to fall, we will await to-morrow before deciding what steps we should take to ensure your safe return. Princes," he added, turning to the chieftains seated around him, "this week we will offer up sacrifices in honour of Ulysses and there will be feasting and games for everyone."

4

The Traveller's Tale

ONG before dawn the palace of Alcinous echoed with the sounds of joyous laughter, whilst the people had gathered together in the market-place, where thrones had been erected for the King, for his guest, and for all the princes of the Phaeacians.

At the feast which followed later in the day, a blind bard took up his lyre and began to sing of the glories of the heroes who conquered Troy, of Agamemnon, Achilles, Menelaus and many others besides. Whilst all the guests applauded, Ulysses hid his face in his cloak and wept bitterly on hearing the names of those he had loved so dearly.

Then, as trumpets were sounded and the games began, the hero watched the prowess of all the athletes.

Finally, a young Phaeacian challenged him to take part in the contests, saying:

"Doubtless you have passed your life tugging an oar, for how else could you stand by and not prove your worth?"

At these words, Ulysses could not restrain his impatience. Leaping into the arena, he showed his skill by surpassing the greatest champions in throwing the javelin and the discus and in wrestling, leaping and running.

When the sun was already low in the western sky, Alcinous ordered the contests to cease, for it was now the hour for the great banquet at which he would receive the winners of the different races. He honoured Ulysses by asking him to sit at his right hand.

"Would it please you, O stranger," said Alcinous, "to hear more songs from the bard—songs that will tell of the last hours of the siege of Troy—for all that we have heard until now has been of the beginning?"

Then, taking up his lyre once more, the bard sang of the great deeds of Ulysses; how he had entered the flanks of the wooden horse; how the Trojans had dragged it into their city; and how the Greeks concealed within it had issued out, opening the gates of Troy to their comrades and setting the town aflame.

"Stranger," said Alcinous, suddenly seizing Ulysses by the hand. "Why these tears upon your face? Why did I see you weep for the death of Achilles this morning? Can it be that some of your kith and kin fell in the course of this famous siege?"

Ulysses rose to his feet and said:

"O King, I am that Ulysses who did not fear to die a death without honour in the dark depths of the wooden horse. I, who love the clash of arms in the light of day, the strife as man to man. I am the Ulysses known for his wiles, but also for his enduring friendships and his devotion to his fatherland."

Cries of astonishment rose up on all sides, and the guests pressed round the hero, whom they wished to touch, to see and to hear. As for Alcinous, he clasped Ulysses to his heart.

"A secret longing drew me to you," said the King. "I felt that a castaway such as you, thrown up naked on our shores, could not fail to be akin to the Immortals. Now tell us, I pray you, the tale of the mishaps which kept you separated from your own land for so many years. Perchance we can find a happy ending to your misfortunes."

"O King, and you, my Phaeacian friends," said Ulysses. "Listen now to the story of my endless wanderings."

Then he told this tale.

As you know full well, no sooner had Troy fallen than dissensions broke out among the Greeks. Therefore, I set out with some, whilst others stayed behind with Agamemnon. The winds first bore us to the Ciconian shores, where, still athirst for plunder, we stormed a city, then feasted heedlessly, so that our foes swept back upon us and caught us unawares. Though our losses were great, we fled to our ships and sailed off across the water again.

Once out at sea, we were caught by the storms. Night after night, we strove against the gales and towering waves, and then at last we were driven into a sheltered anchorage. Alas, scarcely had we dropped anchor than the ambition to depart possessed my mind.

A man as tall as an oak tree, from whose hideous face a single eye stared fiercely at us

We had landed on the shores of the Lotophagi, peaceful folk, whose only nourishment is a flower that grows on the edges of ponds and lakes, a plant which has this peculiarity that whosoever partakes of it forgets forthwith all that has gone before. Some of my warriors persisted in eating some of these lotus flowers, in spite of my counsels, whereupon everything disappeared from their minds and they even forgot their own names. I had to drag them by force back to our ships and, taking advantage of a favourable gust of wind, we hastened away from this perilous land.

However, we were driven by gales towards even greater dangers, for the coast that we reached before sundown was the island of the Cyclops. Never did a pleasanter-seeming land appear before the eyes of storm-tossed mariners. Without digging or ploughing, the fields were covered with barley, wheat and vines, for it seemed that the giants who lived there could rely upon the bounty of the gods to supply them with nourishment.

Our ships had sailed into a sheltered creek on an islet not far from the shores of the land of the Cyclops.

"Let us go and seek out this country," I said to my companions, "and let us see what kind of people inhabit this larger island, for we need to take in stores of water, meat and fruit. We shall discover whether we can do this task without fighting for our needs."

So I selected twelve picked men from my warriors, but a secret presentiment induced me to take with us a goatskin full of the most delicious and heady wine, which I intended to present as a gift to the King of the island in order to gain his favour.

Scarcely had we landed than I saw before me a huge grotto with a vast enclosure before it, whilst the sound of loud bleating struck our ears. "This must be a sheepfold," I said to my companions. "If only we could induce the landowner to sell us the milk and cheese of his sheep and of his goats, we would not need to lose much time in foraging."

So we entered into the sheepfold, and then into the grotto. In both places, the most perfect peace prevailed and it was manifest that the shepherd took the greatest care of his flock.

"We must make the best of this opportunity," said my warriors. "Let us take the plumpest animals, the heaviest baskets of cheese, and let us return swiftly to our comrades in the creek of the islet."

"We must not steal," said I, frowning. "Let us await the return of the shepherd and bargain with him." Scarcely had I finished speaking than a huge shadow was cast over us all, filling up the entrance to the grotto. I turned round and saw before me a man as tall as an oak tree, from whose hideous face a single eye stared fiercely out at us. Concealing the movement of fear and horror that seized me, I duly saluted him.

"In the name of all the gods," I said, "condescend to receive us with kindness. We are Greeks on our way back from Troy, which we reduced to ashes with the approval of Jupiter. We were sailing back to our islands when we were overcome by adverse winds, which cast us up on these unknown shores. We strayed into your dwelling by chance and we were awaiting your coming. . . ."

"Ah, ah," roared the Cyclops with a loud sneer, which

echoed through the cave. "I know only too well why you waited for me. It was to give me a change of food. You have come at the right moment, for I feel the greatest pangs of hunger."

And, before we could stir, he blocked up the entrance to his lair with an enormous rock, and, seizing two of my companions, he crushed them between his fingers, and crunched them up in two mouthfuls. Terrified by this dread spectacle, I uttered a cry of horror and dismay.

"Foolish stranger," he said to me scornfully. "You can know nothing of the dread Cyclops, or you would not prattle to me about the gods. Nonsense such as that can only deceive mortals like you."

Then, turning his back on us, he began to busy himself with his flock.

I seized the hilt of my sword, but what could I have done, even with the help of warriors, against a giant of such prodigious strength? "I shall attack him," I said to my terrified men, "but only when he is fast asleep."

Alas, the entire night passed, whilst the Cyclops sat up, remaining on guard with his only eye fixed on us throughout the hours of darkness. In the morning I had the great sorrow of seeing two more of my comrades captured and devoured.

"Wait until this evening," said the Cyclops with a sneer, and, driving his flock in front of him, he went out, rolling back the rock in front of the entrance of the cave.

I cannot explain to you how great was our horror and distress. We were prisoners, waiting for the most atrocious of deaths. Filled with the deepest distress, I looked around me and suddenly my eyes encountered the goatskin still distended with strong wine.

"Courage," I said to my warriors. "I have found the means of putting this monster into the deepest sleep, but I need some other weapon besides my sword, which is too short for my purpose. We must find something."

It was not long before I discovered in the depth of the grotto the trunk of an olive tree which the giant had felled to serve as his club, for it was large as the mast of a ship. We spent the whole day in shaping it and giving it a sharp point. When the Cyclops returned at nightfall, I approached him boldly.

"I did not tell you," I shouted, so that my voice could reach his ears, "that we have brought with us the most splendid wine which you will like even more than human blood. The sun has made you thirsty. Just taste this vintage, and even you will recognise that, after such a gift, you should spare our lives and set us free."

"Give it to me," said the giant, sitting down. "I like wine. We Cyclops produce it ourselves, but I will tell you if yours is better than ours."

I handed him the goatskin; he raised the mouthpiece up to his lips and took several gulps. His one eye sparkled.

"I have never drunk anything as good," he admitted. "What is your name, my friend?"

"Noman," I replied, concealing my irony with an accent of politeness.

"Well, little Noman," continued the giant, beginning to laugh. "As a reward for your gift, you shall be the last to be devoured. How delicious is this wine! . . ."

I did not reply, for I began to tremble with hope as

I saw his face grow crimson with drunkenness, and I heard his voice begin to falter.

A few minutes later the giant fell fast asleep, and his snoring echoed throughout the grotto.

"Now is the time," I said to my trembling comrades. Five of us lifted up the stake, and we placed the pointed end in a brazier of branches that we had hastily lighted for the purpose. When the wooden extremity was red hot, we turned it carefully towards the head of the monster and at a given sign from me, with the united movement of our arms, we plunged the stake into the eye of the Cyclops.

The latter began to utter such frightful howls that the whole countryside echoed with them. The other Cyclops awakened by his cries, ran up at once. As for ourselves, we hid among the sheep away from the groping hands of the giant.

"What is the matter, Polyphemus?" (for that was his name), asked the Cyclops. "What has happened to you? Who has attacked you?"

"Alas, brothers. Noman," replied the giant with a moan.

"No man, no man," they cried out indignantly. "So you raise the alarm, you disturb us in the middle of the night and no man has done anything to you. You shall not mock us any longer."

From the heavy trampling of feet, we believed that the giants had departed, and I was filled with delight at the happy inspiration which had made me take the name of "Noman".

In vain the Cyclops shouted and called for help, but

not one of his neighbours returned to the cave. Then at
last Polyphemus was inspired with only one thought—
to avenge himself on the man who had blinded him.

We heard him cursing as well as moaning. He rose to
his feet, groped his way to the mouth of the cave, pushed
aside the rock that blocked it, and sat on the threshold in
such a way that his long arms could seize anyone who
tried to go out at the same time as his flock.

Quickly I understood what was happening. Polyphemus was about to take his sheep out to graze, and so
it was of the greatest importance that we should not
allow ourselves to be shut in once more. I tied up the
sturdiest rams in threes, and beneath the middle one I
attached one of my companions, with injunctions to
make himself as small as possible.

All these preparations kept us busy until the dawn.
Therefore, when the Cyclops called out to his sheep, I
had time to think of my own safety. Fortunately, the bell-
wether of the flock was big and very strong. I slipped under his belly, and I clung to his thick fleece. Still moaning,
the Cyclops ran his hands over the backs of the rams,
goats and sheep as they passed in front of him. As the one
which carried me came out last, he stopped it.

"Ram, is it the fury of seeing your master wounded
thus that makes you come out last—you, who always
frolic at the head of the flock? Ah, if only you could speak,
you could tell me in what corner of my cave these scoun-
drels are lurking. If only I could crush that rascally
Noman and hear his screams, I should feel some relief."

As I heard these words, I could not stop myself from
trembling. I felt the enormous hands of the giant groping

over the woolly back of the beast, and then at last I was able to breathe freely, for Polyphemus had released the ram, and, catching up with the rest of the flock, it began to graze in the meadow. Leaping to our feet, and without losing a moment, I and my companions set off for the shore, driving the plumpest sheep in front of us. We did not stop until we reached our ships, on which we embarked without delay.

As we pulled out to sea, I shouted out with all my might:

"Polyphemus, vile monster that you are, your victims have escaped from your clutches. You failed in the sacred duties of hospitality, but the punishment that you received will make you suffer for the rest of your life. You can say to yourself that he who plunged you into the world of darkness was no less than Ulysses, King of Ithaca."

A yell was the reply, for the giant had heard my first words, and was stumbling towards the shore. Once there, he stopped, picked up an enormous rock and flung it in the direction of my voice and he aimed so accurately that he nearly shattered our ship.

"O Father Neptune," cried Polyphemus when he gathered from our scornful laughter that he had missed his target. "Do not allow a mere mortal to make a mockery of your son. May this rascally Ulysses never live to set foot again on his native land, I beseech you, O dread god with the sable locks."

By then our boat had already reached the creek of the green islet where our friends were awaiting us, though the shouts and the insults of the Cyclops still rang in our ears.

We duly sacrificed to the gods to thank them for having preserved us from such peril, and to ask them to speed our return to Ithaca, but Neptune was not moved by our prayers, and his vengeance continued to follow us.

5

The Peril at Sea Continues

AUTIOUSLY, we landed on the shores of Aeolia a few days later, though the welcome we received from the King who was the friend of all the gods should have assured us a safe and speedy return to our beloved Ithaca.

Aeolus had expressed real pity on hearing the sad tale of our wanderings and of the mishaps that had befallen us. Indeed, he was willing to do everything within his power to bring our journey to a happy end.

"Jupiter has appointed me to be lord of the winds," he said. "I will imprison all the stormy blasts in this great jar, leaving out only the breeze that comes in from the west to guide you safely and surely to the land of your fathers. But on no account must you speak of this to your companions."

Alas, I should, perhaps, have been wiser to tell them of the gift that I had received, for whilst I slept their curiosity impelled them to open the jar. Believing, doubtless, that they would find in it treasures of gold or of silver, they unleashed the captive winds. Immediately there arose a storm, so that our ships were driven back towards the coast of Aeolia, into the very port which we had just left.

"You are accursed of the gods," said the King of Aeolia when I related to him what happened, after I had thrown myself at his feet. "I thought that you were merely unfortunate, but now I see that you are indeed hated by the immortal gods. Depart from here with all speed!"

Thus we were forced to venture forth again, weighed down with anxiety and fatigue. The winds appeared to have dropped, and we had to use our oars. The seas were as heavy as molten lead, and the deep silence which hung over the waters oppressed us and filled us with dread forebodings. Indeed, the first time that we put in ashore brought us misfortune for we had come upon the island of the Lestrigons—cruel and rapacious giants—and my own ship barely escaped the slaughter and destruction dealt out to the rest of our fleet. Mourning our lost friends, we continued our journey by rowing, since a dead calm prevailed.

At the end of a fortnight of slow and wearisome navigation of this kind, we reached a beauteous tree-clad island where rippling brooks babbled among the trees. We were tired out and we had used all our stores. We leapt ashore joyfully, with relief in our hearts. Nevertheless, I decided to go forward with caution, for I had not forgotten our fateful adventure with the Cyclops.

I advanced towards a high mountain with slopes coming down to the water's edge and there I tried to find a village, but all that I could perceive were golden rooftops in the centre of a huge forest, and so I hastily came back to my companions.

"I saw an immense palace among trees," I said to them, "but we must not forget the dangers that we have just faced. Let us divide into two parties. I will command the first and Eurylochus shall lead the second, and we will draw lots as to whose group shall be the first to seek out the land."

So it was Eurylochus who was due to set out at the head of twenty-two of our warriors, and, as I looked at them I realised how depleted were the numbers that I commanded since we left Troy, and I began to weep. Before the men left, I besought their leader to be careful and to send me back news of their progress before long.

Then, oppressed by anxiety, I sat down near the shore as the hours passed slowly by.

Suddenly I sat up with a start, for I could hear Eurylochus running towards me, and when he arrived he was pale and breathless.

"Noble Ulysses," he said to me. "I have narrowly escaped with my life, but as for our companions, alas! . . ."

"Speak," I cried, horrorstruck.

"In obedience to your orders, we began to cross the forest. Soon we beheld before us a marble palace of dazzling whiteness and, lying all around in the thickets, wild beasts appeared to be listening, fascinated. But soon we were straining our ears with delight, for there came from the mansions the sound of gentle, melodious singing. Then we perceived near an open window the figure of a woman bending over a loom. Did I say a woman? No woman this, but a goddess, for her face was as lovely as her voice. As soon as she saw us she beckoned to us.

"'Come in,' she said. 'You are welcome to rest and refresh yourselves, for never did mortal come nigh to Circe without forgetting all his woes.'

"Seized with a sudden presentiment, I tried in vain to hold back my companions, but neither my commands nor my pleas would stop them from entering the palace.

"'I will wait for you,' I said to them, 'but come back quickly.'

"Two hours passed, and then three, but not one of them reappeared. I cannot tell what has become of them. They may even be dead. So I hastened back to tell you my story."

"We must find out what has happened," I said, picking up my sword and my bow. "Show me the way, Eurylochus."

"No, Ulysses, I beseech you," he said. "Do not face this danger and force me to follow you. Let us flee with the warriors that remain, for what can courage avail against magic and sorcery?"

"I cannot abandon my comrades without discovering what has become of them," I said, resolutely. "Stay if you will, but I must go, even if I have to go alone."

Before he could begin again his supplications, I strode off into the forest, and whilst I walked, I besought the

gods to come to my help. Suddenly I felt the presence of
someone behind me. I turned round and I saw a young
man of superhuman beauty, who looked at me with a
smile. His feet, with golden wings, scarcely seemed to
touch the ground. I knew at once that I was in the
presence of an Immortal, and so I threw myself down
with my face against the ground.

"Ulysses," he said to me in a mellow voice. "Where
are you going, you rash mortal? Into the palace of Circe
to be bewitched like your men? Do you not know that
they have been changed into swine by that sorceress?
Does not that prospect fill you with horror?"

"O gentlest of gods, with your winged heels. O Mercury," I cried. "I did not know of the dread fate of my
companions, but you must know this. I am their chief,
and it behoves me to make every effort to set them free.
Death alone can bend my will!"

The god smiled.

"You are brave, Ulysses, I know, and if your protection had been able to ward off the anger of Neptune you
would have been home by now. But the protection I am
unable to give you at sea I have power to give you on
land. Take this plant and hide it in your bosom, for with
it the spells and potions of Circe are of no avail. Con-
strain her by oath to set free your companions and to
give you the necessary help to continue your journey.
But I warn you, Ulysses, take heed lest your heart be
ensnared by the wiles of this sorceress."

I promised Mercury to steel myself against the charms
of Circe, and, taking the flower that he proffered me, I
placed it against my heart, and the god disappeared.

When I arrived at the gates of the palace, I soon realised the strength of the spell which had captivated my companions. Never did more enchanting voice echo on this earth, but nevertheless, I called out to Circe in greeting.

"What do you want of me, mortal?" she asked, appearing on the threshold. "Do you wish to lay aside your woes? If so, come in, for Circe will make you forget them."

I obeyed her, but my heart was filled with a strange sadness.

How could so divine a voice and such beauty conceal such evil guile? Tremulously, I pressed the plant against my heart.

"Sit down," said the goddess to me tenderly, "and take this potion. I will dispel all the weariness and sorrows of the past."

Half reclining on the soft pillows of a golden couch, I took the cup and drank. Immediately, Circe struck me with a wand:

"Go," she said to me in a voice full of venom. "Go into the sheds and lie down in the dirt with your companions."

I sat up and placed my hand on the hilt of my sword. Circe started back, uttered a terrible cry, and fell at my knees weeping.

"Who are you?" she sobbed. "And how is it that you have not succumbed to my potion, for no man has been able to withstand me before. Assuredly, you must be Ulysses, the Greek hero whose coming the gods foretold. Do not feel for your sword, noble hero, for I am no longer your foe. Instead, I offer you my heart."

Now the beauty of the sorceress was increased by her tears, but, mindful of the warnings of Mercury, I thrust her back gently.

"Circe," I said to her, feigning great emotion, "How can I place my trust in you, who have treated my comrades so shamefully? If you really wish to gain my trust, you must swear to me by the unbreakable oath of the immortals that you can be true to me."

On hearing this, Circe grew pale and tried to make me desist from my request, but I knew that my safety was at stake and would not relent, so she had to pronounce the fateful words.

"Dear Ulysses," she said after she had sworn the oath, "come and partake of the banquet that awaits me and cast out the thoughts that beset you. All trace of enmity has disappeared between us, so let us rejoice."

"Circe," I replied, "I cannot share your festivities so long as my warriors are wallowing in the mire in the shape of swine. Give them back their manly form. That is the wish of Ulysses!" I added, seeing that the sorceress was about to refuse my request.

A few minutes later my warriors were standing before me, weeping with relief at their emancipation.

"Ulysses," said Circe, "and you, his beloved warriors, weep no more. I would wish that you would stay with me for ever, but I feel that you must leave me now and I grieve, for the most terrible perils await you. The Syrens, seated in the green meadows near the shore, are preparing to lure you into danger with their most captivating songs. Woe to those who listen to them, for they will never return to their homes. Beware of those dangerous creatures, for they have caused the deaths of many a staunch mariner."

So she spoke to me at length, giving me the wisest of counsels and putting me on my guard against the dangers before us. When, at last, she ceased to speak, I turned to my companions:

"Friends," I said, "I know that we are advancing towards the direst peril. Swear that you will obey me without a murmur. First of all, you must bind me firmly to the mast of our craft, and be sure to tie the knots so that I cannot possibly undo them, however much I may beseech you to do so. Take this fragrant wax and stop your ears with it completely. Only in this way can we sail past the great threats that are before us."

My companions soon tied me up as they had been told to do, and then, deaf to every sound, they gripped their oars, and the ship seemed to skim over the waves.

Then suddenly a divine music struck my ears. Seized with a hitherto unknown delight, I listened with straining ears to songs the like of which Circe herself could not have sung. These were the words that I heard:

"Happy the mariners who sail towards these shores, for ne'er will they depart, and our voices will enchant them for eternity. Come, mortals, steep your souls in the unending songs of the Syrens."

"Friends," I implored my men, straining with all my might at the ropes that bound me, "cut my bonds, lay aside your oars, and let us land on these enchanted shores." What mattered Greece to me, my home, my wife, if only I could listen to these voices until death claimed me?

What mattered Greece if only I could listen to these voices?

In vain I besought my comrades, commanding them, wailing and weeping to obtain my desire. They remained at their benches, tugging at their oars, as heedless to my prayers as to those voices of enchantment. Soon the island of death vanished before my eyes, and it seemed to me that I had just awakened from a dream.

"What can that be?" cried Eurylochus suddenly, rising up with horror and pointing to a black column of smoke which rose into the sky.

His movement was noticed by my companions, and all eyes were turned towards the cloud of threatening dust which spread over our heads, and began to fall on us in a warm, dusky shower. In a trice they had cut my bonds and had taken the wax out of their ears.

"Noble Ulysses," they cried, "this poisonous cloud of smoke will choke us and cause our deaths."

"No," said I. "Circe has told me how to avoid the attacks of the monster whom we are about to pass. He can do us no injury unless we arouse still further the wrath of the gods. Your safety lies in doing everything that I tell you to do."

They promised me implicit obedience. Then I took up the tiller again, and, with the help of Eurylochus, I steered our ship away from this danger.

In front of us the sea closed into narrow straits guarded on one side by a monster whose six mouths vomited out ashes and flames, and on the other by a rock which did not project far out of the waves, but had nevertheless a sinister aspect. Indeed, in this place, the waters swirled round in a vast whirlpool that was hollow in the centre. It seemed like a huge jaw waiting to swallow the rippling waves. Now, Circe had told me the names of these reefs, and she had also explained to me how to avoid them.

I steered my craft quite near to the roaring Scylla, so as to keep as far away as possible from the yawning gulf of Charybdis that threatened to drag us down into the furthest depths of the sea. Finally, we had edged past the whirling eddies and our ship glided, once more, through smooth waters.

"Land," cried Eurylochus suddenly with great joy.

My heart contracted. I knew all about this golden and fertile land. Circe had whispered its name to me, and I was fully aware of the danger that awaited us there—a peril that was all the greater, since we needed to control ourselves and our appetites in order to surmount it. Alas, there are monsters harder to master than either Scylla or Charybdis.

"Let us not dally here," I said beseechingly, when I saw my comrades dropping their oars with cries of joy. "Death awaits us here. Of this I am certain. My friends, be sure to keep your solemn oath to obey me."

I wept. I seized hold of their hands imploringly. I besought them in the name of everything they held most dear to hearken to my demand not to land on this alluring island of the sun. Poor fools, they listened to my prayers with impatience and with irony.

"Hold your tongue," cried Eurylochus. "Even though we are worn out with hunger and fatigue, you have to keep us nailed to our benches! You are relentless and without pity. If we could eat and drink our fill, we should recover our strength. See! It is already late, so we could sleep. The night was made for repose; to use it otherwise is to arouse the anger of the gods."

In vain I continued to beseech my men, but all my comrades had applauded the words of Eurylochus.

"At least," I begged when I found that I could not restrain them, "promise me that, if you come upon any flocks or herds you will leave them alone, for they belong to the sun, and if his anger were aroused, it would be fatal."

"I will indeed pledge my word, and that of all my companions not to touch a single beast," replied Eurylochus. "We have supplies of wine and grain, so why should we covet flocks that do not belong to us?"

So, somewhat reassured, I gave my consent to their departure.

Since heavy black clouds had gathered on the horizon and the waves were beginning to rise, we drew up our boat on to the beach, and then went to sleep.

During the night a formidable tempest arose and the next day and for many days that followed the wind blew hard and mountainous waves swept over the sea. A whole month passed in this wise, and at first my companions rejoiced at being under shelter.

Little by little, idleness began to oppress them. Our stores diminished rapidly and we had to fish and to hunt in order to obtain food. As for me, I scoured the countryside in the hopes of finding inhabitants who would be prepared to succour us.

One day, on returning from one of these expeditions, I heard joyous songs echoing near the shore and saw smoke rising from an immense fire. Then my nostrils caught the smell of roast meat, and immediately the thought came into my mind that my men must have killed sheep and oxen taken from among the herd and flocks grazing nearby.

"We are doomed," I said to myself sorrowfully.

The warriors greeted me with a certain uneasiness.

"We have nothing to fear," they said at once, "for, before beginning this repast, we offered up a sacrifice to the gods."

"Alas!" I sighed. "Nothing can save us now."

"Our hunger was greater than our fear," said Eurylochus, his mouth full of the delicious food. "Let us eat, and then set sail as soon as possible. In this way we will escape the wrath of the owner of these flocks."

I refused to share in their feast. Throughout the night, I besought the gods not to punish these perfidious men. The next day the sea was calm, the sky was clear and everything appeared to be favourable for our departure.

"Ulysses," cried Eurylochus, "you harried us needlessly. The gods are on our side."

Within a few minutes we had put to sea, and with the help of our oars and a strong supporting breeze, we were soon far from land.

Suddenly the sky was overcast, the rain began to fall in torrents and a howling gale snapped off our mast and tore away our sails, whilst the swiftly-rising waves carried away our oars, driving the ship ever onwards. In spite of their efforts to cling to the hull, my comrades were thrown into the sea, whilst I had only time to take hold on a spar and, invoking the help of the gods, I was forced to let myself drift at the mercy of the surging waters.

From Scylla to Charybdis, from Charybdis to Scylla, hour after hour, I was cast from one side to the other of the straits, until at last a strong current carried me away and cast me upon the shores of Calypso's Isle.

6

The Secret Return to Ithaca

LYSSES then came to the end of his story and the guests looked at him with eyes full of pity.

"Noble King of Ithaca," said Alcinous at last. "We are moved with compassion for all the misfortunes that you have endured with such valour. The best that we can do is to help you to forget your sufferings by lavishing gifts upon you, so that you do not arrive in your own land empty-handed."

The next day at dawn, Ulysses set out to sea in the ship lent to him by the Phaeacians, but, wearied by all his past emotions, he slept without even counting the passing of the hours. The light shock of the keel grinding on a sandy shore waked him at last and he sat up and looked around him. Before him rose the mountains of his native land. Nearby, he saw the harbour from which he had so often sailed, the fields where his flocks had grazed, the grotto from which flowed cool springs of clear water.

Ulysses knelt on the beach, weeping with delight, but the Phaeacian crew were anxious to return home, so they landed the gifts which their King had given the Greek hero and stowed them away in the grotto. Having done this, they embarked and sailed away.

Rolling a rock to close the entrance of the cave, so as to safeguard his treasures, Ulysses sat down in the shade of an olive tree and pondered. Suddenly he started up. A young man who looked like a shepherd, but whose dazzling glance revealed him to be Minerva in earthly guise, laid his hand on the hero's shoulder.

"Ulysses," she said, "more than ever do you need to be cautious. For more than four years, a number of suitors have occupied your palace in the hope of forcing Penelope to choose one of their number as a husband. They have, of course, plundered your property, but you must not think that you can attack them, for they are too numerous, and they would kill you. Resort to cunning, therefore, for it is often mightier than force. Go to Eumaeus, your faithful swineherd, but first of all I must give you a disguise.

"I will give you white hair, cover your face with wrinkles and clothe you in rags, so that the King of Ithaca will seem to be only a beggar who can approach his enemies and even his family without being recognised. Whilst you are staying with Eumaeus, I will go and fetch Telemachus, whom I sent to Sparta so that the whole of Greece should learn the worth of your son. Soon you will be able to embrace him, even though his enemies have prepared an ambush. Fools that they are! They think that they can counter the will of Minerva and attack her wards."

Ulysses knelt before the goddess to thank her, and then swiftly his appearance was transformed by her spell. When he rose to his feet, he was old and bent, his eyes were dull and misted; he held a stick in his trembling hand and from his shoulder hung a torn sack.

The goddess then flew off to Sparta, whilst Ulysses remained alone.

Slowly, he left the beach, and walked through shady groves to the hut where dwelt Eumaeus, wisest and most faithful of his former servants.

The sheds once filled with swine and plump sheep were now almost empty, for every day the suitors forced Eumaeus to send pigs or lambs to the palace for their feasts.

As Ulysses approached the cottage, the watch-dogs came out to bark and ran up to him, but Eumaeus called them back.

"What do you want, old man?" he cried. "Doubtless you need food. Welcome to my dwelling! Each time that some beggar comes to my door, I ask myself if it could be our good king, starving and weary, and this thought makes me feel more strongly the call of hospitality. Sit down. I can give you but little, for the wealth of my master's house has departed. I see the day coming when our sheds will be empty."

Tears coursed down the cheeks of the swineherd, but he hastened to set some meat before the vagrant and filled a cup of wine for him.

"My master, Ulysses, was rich," explained Eumaeus sadly, "when he sailed for Troy to fight for King Agamemnon and his family. There were large herds of cattle and countless flocks of sheep and goats in the fields of Epirus, but all this wealth is diminishing rapidly, for the chieftains are consuming it in feasting. Doubtless they believe that he is dead. Otherwise they would not dare to do this and to oppress his faithful servants."

"Do you regret your master?" said Ulysses with emotion.

"Do I regret him?" said Eumaeus in a faltering voice. "He was the kindest and most merciful of men, and the wisest of kings."

"My friend," replied Ulysses, "I call great Jupiter to witness that you will soon see your master again. By the end of this month he will have come back to his palace and will have driven away the suitors, and prosperity will return to this land."

Eumeaus shook his head sadly.

"Let us hope that you speak the truth, but how can I believe this after so many years of waiting? Who may you be that you promise the return of our King with such certainty? Have you seen him, and if so, where? Speak, venerable old man—tell me whence you come?"

"I am from Crete and my father's name was Castor," said Ulysses, for he did not wish Eumaeus to recognise him. "I have had news of your King—he sought the oracle at Dodona to ask whether it would be better to return openly to Ithaca or arrive by stealth."

Eumaeus raised up his arms in astonishment. "You are mocking me, you old dotard," he cried. "All that you tell me about Ulysses is unbelievable and you are trying to lead me astray with your falsehoods. I beseech you, do not attempt to allay my sorrow with these tales."

"You must not doubt my word," said Ulysses with a smile. "Will you take a wager with me? If your master does return here before the month is out, as I have promised you, you must give me a tunic and cloak to replace these rags. If he be not here in time, let your shepherds throw me down from the top of this steep cliff for my lies."

Eumaeus, really impressed, began to look at the supposed beggar with fear, and he invited him to sit down and share a shin of pork with him. They feasted all day until sunset, and then Eumaeus offered Ulysses his own couch to sleep on whilst he wrapped himself in a goatskin and lay down on some straw in the stables.

Meanwhile, Minerva had flown off to Sparta and had approached the sleeping Telemachus.

"Awake," she said, "for day is about to dawn, and you must set off without delay for Ithaca. Your mother's father and brothers are trying to force her to marry Eurymachus, the most powerful and the richest of her suitors. Nevertheless, in spite of the need for haste, you must proceed with caution, for your enemies have prepared an ambush in the Straits of Ithaca and in the rocks of Same. You must go at night by a devious route and land on the south coast near the house of Eumaeus, your father's chief herdsman. You will lodge there, whilst he goes to inform Penelope of your arrival, but you must hasten."

The young Prince leapt up, dressed and wakened his

friend, Pisistratus, and together they set off in the chariot with the horses at a full gallop.

The next day at sunset, they drove into the port of Pylos, where Telemachus embarked in his ship, after bidding his friend an affectionate farewell.

Then the crew bent over their oars, a favourable wind sent by Minerva filled the sail, and the vessel glided smoothly through the darkness of the night without mishap. Just before dawn, Telemachus landed on the shores of Ithaca, and with joyous tread began to climb the slopes leading to the house of Eumaeus. As he approached, the dogs heard his footsteps and rushed out to meet him.

"Eumaeus," said Ulysses, who was sitting near the herdsman, "what has befallen the dogs? I thought that they were heralding the arrival of a stranger, but they are barking joyously as if to greet the newcomer."

Eumaeus went to the door and uttered a cry of delight. "Beloved Prince and son," he cried. "I never thought to see you again, for the thought of your departure for Pylos filled me with despair. It was as though I had lost my beloved master, Ulysses, a second time."

"Dear friend," replied Telemachus, "I also am happy to see you once more. I did not wish to return directly to Ithaca, for I would learn from you first what had been happening in my absence. Has my mother at last given way to her father and promised to accept one of the suitors?"

"How can you thus misunderstand your wise and faithful mother?" said Eumaeus, reproachfully. "She never leaves the women's quarters and her days are spent in mourning for her husband. Now, noble Prince, you see before you an old Cretan, whom I would beg you to take under your care."

"I can give him clothing, and one of my ships can take him back to his own country," replied Telemachus. "But how can I lodge him in my palace? My mother's suitors are the masters there, and I fear that they would insult this venerable old man."

"Great Prince, forgive my questions," said Ulysses with assumed humility, "but why must you bow down under this hateful yoke? It seems to me that if I were the son of Ulysses, or Ulysses himself back from his long wanderings, I should stand firm against the demands of these importunate intruders, and I would triumph over them. You are strong and you are young. This spear which I see in your hand is meant for battle. I would rather die than endure the insults of these pretentious men."

"O aged one," replied Telemachus, "I have often reproached myself for inaction, but there are battles which cannot be fought without disaster. My palace is occupied by a host of suitors. From Dulichium alone there came fifty-two chieftains: Twenty-four arrived from Same; twenty more from Zacynthe were joined by at least twelve from Ithaca itself; and each of them brought an army of servants, cooks and musicians. If I did attack these vile intruders, I should be killed by them and my mother would be left with no one at all to protect her. That is why, for all these years, I have been forced to submit to insults and humiliation.

"Eumaeus," continued the young Prince. "Go to

Ithaca forthwith. Tell my mother that I have returned, and try to find out if I can go to my palace without endangering my life."

Whilst the herdsman hurried away on his mission, Telemachus turned his gaze towards the Cretan beggar and, to his great surprise, he saw before him, not a white-haired old man with withered skin and bent back, but a tall, strong warrior, with dark hair and youthful vigour.

The young man thought that he was in the presence of a god from Olympus, and he stammered respectfully: "Who may you be, O stranger? What sudden change has so transformed your body? If you are an Immortal, bring me back my father, I pray you."

"Telemachus, my well-beloved son," declared Ulysses, opening his arms to him, "I am no god. I am your father, whom you have mourned so greatly, and who has suffered so much, far away from all those who loved him. Let us give thanks to the gods, and most of all to our kindly Minerva," continued Ulysses, "for they have succoured us and brought us together, and they will no longer keep us apart. Now we must strive against these presumptuous intruders in our palace. Go there to-morrow. Try to find out which of our servants and our slaves have remained faithful to us, and which have been won over by our foes.

"Say not a word about my return, and when you do see me do not let anyone discover that the dirty old beggar is of interest to you. Even if, perchance, I am ill-treated, you must remain unmoved. I know that this may be hard for you, but, believe me, cunning is our strongest weapon."

7

The Beggar at the Palace

ONG before the sun had reached its zenith in the heavens, Telemachus had arrived at his palace. He had left Ulysses, now a bent old man again, in the care of Eumaeus. The latter had brought back word from the city that Antinous intended to kill the Prince in his own palace, as the ambush had failed.

So Telemachus hastened on that his enemies might not have time to plot against him in his absence.

On seeing the young Prince, Antinous approached and said with an evil smile: "I am glad to see you, Telemachus, for I had feared that you had been assailed by a storm at sea."

"You cannot tell how dear you are to us," added Eurymachus with a false glance. "I was awaiting your return with impatience."

Telemachus thanked his treacherous friends for their kindness, and joined Mentor, Antiphus and Haliserthes —old and tried friends of his father, in whose company he felt safe.

He invited them to sit beside him at the banquet in the Great Hall, where the suitors gathered every day to eat baked meats, vegetables and fruit.

Whilst songs and bursts of laughter echoed in the rafters, Telemachus listened, though his heart was heavy within him. In the meantime, Ulysses followed Eumaeus into the city, walking as fast as his apparent age would allow him.

In his joy at seeing once more the familiar places that he had known long ago, Ulysses dallied for a while near a fountain whose clear waters he had been wont to drink on hot summer's days.

"We must move on with all speed," said Eumaeus, suddenly, "for here comes Melanthus, son of Dolius, the idlest and wickedest man possible, and attached, moreover, to the wretched men who intrude into the palace of our king. He is a goatherd, but that does not prevent him from making free with the flocks of our absent master."

"O Eumaeus," cried Melanthus with coarse laughter. "Where are you taking that dirty old beggar, you foolish, stupid shepherd? He has an ugly, rascally face, and someone will break a stick over his head when he gets to the palace. In the meantime, he can take this . . ."

And approaching Ulysses, Melanthus gave him a great kick in the ribs and then went on his way, still laughing loudly. In his wrath, Eumaeus would have run after the goatherd and made him pay dearly for his brutality, but Ulysses restrained him.

"That blustering goatherd will get his due in time," he said. "Do not think any more about him, and let us continue on our way. But what is this poor creature that I see rooting in the manure? Ah, it is a dog. How thin he is! Surely he must be a stray abandoned by his master?"

"No," said Eumaeus, "it is old age that gives him this sorry look, for once he belonged to Ulysses, who is far from us now. The slaves who should tend him do not feed poor Argus. . . ."

"Argus," cried Ulysses with emotion. But then he was silent and turned away his head. How many times had he set out, spear in hand, to hunt the boar or the stag with the same hound by his side!

On hearing his name spoken, Argus sat up, for he knew this voice, even though it had not called out to him for so many years. No sooner did he set eyes on his beloved master than he gave one great spasm and died.

"I must seek my vengeance," thought Ulysses, and, restraining his tears, he walked into the banqueting hall.

"Who is this filthy fellow?" said Eurymachus when he perceived him. "Was there ever a more hideous beggar? Next to him, Irus becomes the handsomest of men. Irus, my friend," he called out to a huge and hairy beggar who sat by the threshold. "You are strong. You must rid us of this idle rascal. If you fight it out, the winner shall have a side of goat's meat as a prize."

Urged on and incited in this way, Irus rushed towards

Ulysses, but the latter straightened himself up and gave his attacker a mighty blow of his fist and felled him to the ground. Then the hero dragged him out of the hall by his feet, and set him up against a wall.

"Do not dare to venture again into the King's palace," said Ulysses. "You are not even fit to gather up the food that falls from his table."

Then the hero returned to the banqueting hall.

"You are strong, my friend," said Eurymachus, laughing. "and fully you deserve the reward of victory, so you shall have it. See, take this goat's shin and see if it is not too tough for your shaky old teeth!"

The other suitors followed the example of Eurymachus and pressed alms on the old beggar, whilst Telemachus watched with anxious eyes to see if his father would receive all these gifts with due humility. When Ulysses came up to Antinous, the latter thrust him back roughly.

"You wretched old spoil-sport, go and display your tawdry rags elsewhere, but if you must have alms, you shall have them."

And, picking up a wooden stool, he threw it at the old man's head.

The latter moved slightly to one side and was only struck in the shoulder, but, in spite of the shock he did not wince, and looked at Antinous with such fury that the latter paused for a while, and then, regaining his courage, he began to hurl insults and abuse at the beggar. Then did Telemachus rise to his feet and say, "Antinous, take heed. You are in my palace. This man is my guest and I will not let anyone insult him."

At these words, most of the suitors began to laugh in the

most insolent manner, though there were a few of their number who tried to restrain them.

Aroused by the noise, Penelope came into the Great Hall with two of her handmaidens.

"Why these cries, my lord?" she asked Antinous. "Who has aroused your ire?"

Contemptuously, the suitor pointed to Ulysses, who was sitting with bowed head.

"Behold the fine guest that your son has tried to impose on us, O Queen," he said. "Were it not for your beauty, Telemachus would have paid for his insolence with bloodshed."

"My son," said Penelope, seizing the Prince by the hand. "How is it that you can sit at the same table as these people? How can you, the son of one of the greatest of Greek heroes, allow one of your guests to be insulted in your presence?"

"O wise Penelope," said Eurymachus respectfully, "I welcome these dissensions, for they have brought you into our midst that we may admire your beauty."

"My beauty departed when Ulysses left for Troy," replied Penelope, "and it will only return when he is once more in his kingdom."

"Why so sad, O Queen?" cried Antinous. "Was it not the wish of Ulysses himself that you should take another husband if he should die in battle, and so soon as you should come of age? That day has come, so why defer your choice?"

"Can there be one among you worthy of my hand?" said Penelope disdainfully. "Those who seek a woman in marriage do not, as a rule, bring havoc and desolation to her house. Rather do they show their generosity with splendid gifts. Yet here there is nothing but plunder and looting."

At these words the suitors were overcome with shame, and despatched their servants to bring back presents for Penelope.

Whilst she sat alone, pondering over her woes, Ulysses approached her, though little did she guess that this white-haired beggar was the husband she was mourning so grievously.

"Queen," said the old man with the greatest humility, "if you will permit me to speak to you when the guests have gone and this palace is empty, I will give you news of Ulysses, whereby I can help to allay the woes that oppress you now."

Though she could scarcely believe her ears, she nodded in assent, and then rose to go to her private apartments. When she had left, Telemachus went up to Antinous and said: "Prince, night is falling, so we cannot continue our feasting without giving offence to the gods. Let us, therefore, seek repose in sleep and meet again to-morrow."

"No," replied Antinous harshly. "Why should I obey a stripling like you? There is yet time for roistering. Let Penelope return here and choose a husband from among us. I will not leave until she has done so."

But Eurymachus and some of his friends intervened, insisting that they were prepared to wait until the morrow.

So, in spite of his protests, Antinous was led away, and Telemachus remained in the hall with the false beggar.

"My son," whispered Ulysses, "let us make the best

of this time. Take down all these weapons that are hanging on the walls and hide them in a secret place. To-morrow, if any of the suitors ask you what has become of them, you will reply that they were being rusted and tarnished by the smoke of the feasting, and that you feared, moreover, that if quarrels arose in the heat of wine, someone might be tempted to bloodshed by the sight of them. I pray you summon Euryclea and bid her close firmly the women's quarters lest any slave should see what we are doing. Go now to your rest, my son. You will need all your strength for to-morrow's strife."

Whilst Ulysses remained alone in the hall, Penelope came up to him to ask him for news of her husband.

"Speak," she said with impatience. "Have pity on my anxious heart. Tell me what you know of Ulysses."

Then in a low voice, the hero unfolded the story of his long imprisonment on Calypso's isle; of how his companions had been drowned when trying to pass Scylla and Charybdis, of the friendly welcome that he had received from the Phaeacians. He related all these things as if he, the Cretan beggar, had learnt them from the mouth of Ulysses himself, and he assured Penelope that her husband was at hand and would soon deliver her from the importunate wooing of her many suitors.

"Kindly father," said Penelope, seizing the false beggar by the hands, "from henceforth you are to be the honoured guest of this house. Euryclea," she added, turning to the old nurse, "bring out the richest tunic, bathe the feet of our aged friend. To-morrow you shall feast with Telemachus himself."

Then Euryclea knelt before the beggar, and placed on

the floor next to him a basin full of scented water, although Ulysses tried in vain to refuse this act of homage. Many years previously, a wild boar had wounded one of his knees with a deep lunge of its tusks, and in washing his feet Euryclea would not fail to see the well-known scar. So it was that the hero tried to keep her away, but the old nurse persisted. There was something in the hero's voice and bearing that reminded her of her lost master, and then, at last, her fingers found the fatal scar.

"Do not speak," whispered Ulysses, placing his hand over the mouth of Euryclea, who could scarce control her joy. "Yes, I am Ulysses, but you must be silent and keep my secret for a while."

"I would rather die than betray you," said the nurse. "May the gods give you victory over all your enemies."

"Venerable old man," said Penelope, coming up slowly. "I have had such joy in speaking to you that I would seek your counsel. As you well know, I have been hard-pressed by my presumptuous suitors, but to-morrow, alas, I must make my choice, for my son has given his oath that I should do so.

"Think, then how great is my anguish and perplexity. Ulysses is at hand, but were I to proclaim it how great would be his peril. This, then, is what I have conceived. No man on earth is as strong and as skilful as Ulysses; no one but he can bend his bow, or shoot so unerringly through twelve rings. Thus will I say that I will take as husband he who can bend this bow and let fly twelve arrows through these rings. May the gods grant that my hopes are not ill-placed and that no one can vie with Ulysses."

"Be reassured, O Queen," said Ulysses, delighted with this stratagem. "Before any of these idle suitors of yours can bend this bow and prove their skill at archery, Ulysses will be here by your side."

So firm was his voice, and so convincing his tone, that Penelope set off for her couch, to sleep peacefully until the next day.

*   *   *

When dawn had climbed on to her golden throne, Ulysses arose to pray to Jupiter and to Minerva to grant him their support throughout the trials of the coming day.

Already the slaves were lighting fires to prepare for the feast, crushing grain and cutting up the meat that was to be roasted slowly on great spits. Each was given an allotted task, and among them came Philetus, a tried and trusted servant of the King in years gone by. On seeing Ulysses, the beggar, past memories stirred within him and he cried: "I thought that I saw Ulysses before my eyes. Alas, my poor King! Perchance he wanders thus naked, old and friendless before his time."

"You may set your mind at rest," replied the beggar. "You will soon see your master again, but in the meantime all that I ask of you is that throughout this day you stay near to me and to your young Prince."

Soon the suitors crowded into the palace, and the feasting began with much drinking and ribald laughter. Though Telemachus invited him to sit down at table by his side, Ulysses refused, and crouched on the ground near the door, in all humility.

8

The Return of Ulysses

"AGABONDS like this beggar should not be present at our feast," cried Antinous, looking angrily at Ulysses. "Take this, my fine wedding guest, and may it choke you."

With these words, he snatched up a shin of beef and threw it with all his might at Ulysses, who avoided it with a dextrous twist of his head. Antinous was about to renew his attack on the beggar, but Eurymachus held him back.

"Let us not continue the ridiculous quarrels that we began yesterday," he said. "We are here for one purpose only—that Penelope should decide which of us she is to take as husband. I cannot tell why, but I feel in no mood for jesting. I am possessed of sad thoughts, and it seems that death is casting a shadow over this hall."

"You are either very foolish or mad," said Antinous

roughly. "There is no place for death in this joyous feasting, though Penelope is slow in joining us. Slaves, tell your mistress that we await her coming, and that we are weary of her weeping and mourning."

When Penelope came at last, she held in her hand the mighty bow which Iphitus of Messenia gave Ulysses in time past by. Her women slaves followed, bearing a golden quiver full of sharp arrows and a bronze casket containing twelve silver rings.

"Prince and chieftains, listen to my words," said the Queen majestically. "You have all aspired to wed me and to fill the throne of Ulysses. I have long resisted your pretensions, for I felt that not one of you could equal his great virtues. Yet now that I am forced by my father's will and your persistence to give my hand to one of you, I wish to choose a man who is in no way inferior in strength and in skill to my first husband. Since you can never vie with the intelligence and kindness of this great hero, I am prepared to submit to the one of you who will equal him in strength and muscle. The suitor who can bend this bow and shoot his swift arrows through these rings I will choose as a husband."

"Ah," cried Telemachus, who did not know what had passed between Ulysses and Penelope. "Let me try my hand at this. If I succeed, my mother shall not leave the palace."

So saying, he stripped off his cloak, and dug a long trench in the courtyard, in which his slaves planted stakes. To these, he tied the rings through which the arrows were to be shot. Then thrice he tried to bend the bow, but each time the string slipped from his fingers.

Full of ardour, he was about to make a fourth attempt when his eyes fell upon his father and he saw from his glance that he wished him to desist.

"I am too young," he admitted. "I cannot do it. Now you prove your skill," and he handed the bow to Eurymachus. The latter grasped it eagerly, and tried to bend it, but in vain. At each attempt his arms fell powerless to his side amid the ironic cheers of the onlookers. Each of the suitors thought that he would be more successful, but each in his turn failed.

"Melanthus," ordered Antinous of a goatherd. "Bring some fat and warm the bow to make it flexible. Antynomus, show us your strength."

In spite of all his efforts, Antynomus failed like all the others, and Ulysses could scarce conceal his joy.

"Let us give up this foolish contest," said Antinous, who had been the last to try in vain to master the mighty weapon. "No mortal could bend this bow, save only great Mars, the god of war, himself."

At these words, Ulysses came forward, and, turning to Telemachus, he asked: "Will you allow me to try my luck, O Prince?"

At once cries of fury and mockery rose up on all sides. Antinous, overcome with anger at seeing this ragged beggar trying to rival him, was about to draw his sword and strike him down, but his companions held him back.

"You can kill him later on," they said with jeers as they prepared to watch the downfall and humiliation of the aged beggar.

Without an effort, he bent his bow, and then, taking

an arrow from the quiver, he fitted it to the string and aimed. His shaft flew through all the rings without touching them, then with a gesture, he beckoned to his servants, Eumaeus and Philitus, to close the doors. Recognising their master, they obeyed him with all speed.

Holding his bow, Ulysses turned towards the astonished suitors and said: "And now let us see if I can strike a target that no other man has yet pierced? It may be that Apollo, the divine archer, will speed my arrows."

"Friends," cried Antinous, "what is this madman saying? Let us crush him, strangle him, tear him apart."

Then he rushed forward, but Ulysses had raised again his mighty bow and had let fly an arrow which struck the boastful suitor full in the throat, wounding him so deeply that he fell to the ground, streaming with blood.

At once havoc and tumult arose throughout the palace. Most of the guests had come without their arms and so they ran to seize those which usually hung on the walls of the Great Hall, but in vain, for all the weapons had been taken away by Eumaeus. Thus Ulysses began the swift slaughter of the suitors, shooting off his arrows straight and fast, dealing out death at every shot until the cries of agony echoed through the vaults of the hall and the flagstones ran with blood.

By the hero's side stood Telemachus, Eumaeus and Philitus, felling with their javelins those of the suitors who dared to attack Ulysses.

"Unworthy chieftains," cried the latter in a thunderous voice. "Can it be that you have not recognised me? I am Ulysses, master of this house. What are you doing in my palace? Now I shall despatch you to the land of the dead.

There you may tell the warriors who have fallen gloriously in battle how much you envy their fate. Cowards! You are being slaughtered like sheep for sacrifice!"

In the meantime, Telemachus and Eumaeus, seeing that Ulysses was lacking arrows, brought him some javelins, which he threw with unerring aim. The last survivor of the hecatomb, Leodes, implored Ulysses for mercy, but nothing would check the fury of the hero which flowed on like a rushing torrent no obstacle can stem. So Leodes died also, and fell back on the flagstones among the bodies of lifeless friends, and the last of the suitors had paid the penalty for his presumption.

"Telemachus," said Ulysses to his son, "now that you are safe, and that I also have been spared by the gods, I cannot regret this slaughter. For were these not evil men who sought our death, and so Jupiter has seen fit to punish them?"

"Father," said Telemachus, "what will the people say when they see the slain bodies of those who were the sons and brothers of the mightiest chieftains in Ithaca? By now the tumult must have brought alarm to the city. What are we to do if the palace is besieged? How can we fight against so many?"

"Let the slaves carry away the dead; let them wash the floors and set this hall in order. To-morrow, I shall know how to silence those who dare to raise their voices. My son, with this right arm I vanquished Troy, a city of great heroes. Surely I need not fear the onslaught of a handful of shepherds. If you are afraid, open wide these gates, for then I will face the populace of Ithaca this very day rather than to-morrow."

Ulysses stood on the threshold of his palace. By now Minerva had given back to him his wondrous beauty and his majestic aspect, and he seemed to those who looked upon him one of the greatest of the Immortals. When the people had gathered together, full of awe and great wonder, they recognised the man who had once been their King and had now returned to his throne. Nevertheless, when they beheld the dead, bloodstained bodies of their kinsmen and their friends, cries and lamentations rose up on all sides.

"Silence!" shouted Ulysses in a loud voice. "The ghosts of those you mourn are now assembled on the banks of the Styx, and this is what I hear them saying: 'Our punishment was a just one, decreed by the gods. It was they who brought Ulysses out of the depths of oblivion and armed his vengeance against us. Let us have no more cries; set aside your wrath. All that we ask of you is your tears, to speed us on our journey to the Elysian Fields.' So, my people, you must learn to submit to the will of the gods."

Though all the listeners grew pale at this pronouncement, Eupithes, father of Antinous, came forward with upraised fist.

"Murderous King," he cried, "you have killed my son and you dare to say, 'The gods are on my side.' How can you prove this to me? You make bold to appear before us still covered with the blood of our sons, and you ask us to applaud your crimes? That can never be! Death which you eluded in the fields of Troy awaits you here, and it shall be at my hands!"

Eupithes rushed towards Ulysses, spear in hand, but

the hero stepped aside. His opponent was carried forward and transfixed on the hero's outthrust sword.

"It is the decree of the gods," said Mentor in a loud voice, "Ulysses is under their protection and Minerva herself must be by his side."

At this moment, as if to increase still further the fear that possessed the hearts of the people, there was a roar of thunder, and blinding forked lightning flashed across the summer sky, for it seemed as if great Jupiter himself wished to express the wrath that he would feel for the people of Ithaca if they should counter his wishes.

All signs of resistance vanished. Slowly and silently, the onlookers filed away, taking with them their dead.

Ulysses stood for a while, motionless and silent, overcome by the thought of the anger of his subjects, which he had mastered with the help of the gods. As ever, he had been able to face the threat of death and destruction, and now he seemed to be outside the realm of human passions.

"Father," said Telemachus, approaching the hero respectfully, "we must return to the palace, for Euryclea has told my mother that you were coming."

But as they spoke they saw Penelope approach with pale face and lowered eyes. "Can this truly be Ulysses?" she asked in a trembling voice.

"Yes, my dear mistress," replied Euryclea, weeping, "this is certainly our King."

Penelope looked up at the hero with doubt mingled with suspicion in her gaze.

"I have waited so long," she murmured. "Can it really be he?"

"O wife," said Ulysses with eyes full of joyous tears, "I admired your beauty in the past, but now I am proud to see you so confident, so faithful, so courageous and yet so wise. At this moment I feel that my twenty long years of strife and of suffering have not been spent in vain—if I can find such virtues on my return."

"It is true that you possess the voice and the features of my lost husband," affirmed Penelope, "but tell me just one thing that he alone could have known, so that I may be sure of making no error."

"Well," said Ulysses, "you must tell our slaves to prepare for us the bed that I carved from a sturdy old olive tree and inlaid with silver and gold with my own hands. My well-beloved, no man can know of this but me. Come, let us go and sleep in it with peace in our souls and joy in our hearts, for the long years of separation and tribulation are at an end."